# Maintaining the Balance Between Manpower, Skill Levels, and PERSTEMPO

Raymond E. Conley, Albert A. Robbert, Joseph G. Bolten, Manuel Carrillo, Hugh G. Massey

Prepared for the United States Air Force

Approved for public release; distribution unlimited

PROJECT AIR FORCE

The research described in this report was sponsored by the United States Air Force under Contract F49642-01-C-0003 and FA7014-06-C-0001. Further information may be obtained from the Strategic Planning Division, Directorate of Plans, Hq USAF.

**Library of Congress Cataloging-in-Publication Data**

Conley, Raymond E.
    Maintaining the balance between manpower, skill levels, and PERSTEMPO /
Raymond E. Conley, Albert A. Robbert, [et al.].
      p. cm.
    "MG-492."
    "RAND Project AIR FORCE."
    Includes bibliographical references.
    ISBN-13: 978-0-8330-3951-4 (pbk. : alk. paper)
      1. United States. Air Force—Personnel management. I. Robbert, Albert A.,
1944– II. Title.

UG773.C65 2006
358.4'1610973—dc22

                                                                    2006027313

The RAND Corporation is a nonprofit research organization providing objective analysis and effective solutions that address the challenges facing the public and private sectors around the world. RAND's publications do not necessarily reflect the opinions of its research clients and sponsors.

**RAND**® is a registered trademark.

Published 2006 by the RAND Corporation
1776 Main Street, P.O. Box 2138, Santa Monica, CA 90407-2138
1200 South Hayes Street, Arlington, VA 22202-5050
4570 Fifth Avenue, Suite 600, Pittsburgh, PA 15213-2665
RAND URL: http://www.rand.org/
To order RAND documents or to obtain additional information, contact
Distribution Services: Telephone: (310) 451-7002;
Fax: (310) 451-6915; Email: order@rand.org

# Preface

This monograph describes research into the U.S. Air Force's manpower, personnel, and training system and current personnel tempo (PERSTEMPO) issues. It discusses this system and how it functions and makes suggestions about how it might be improved in the future. To illustrate some of the interactions, it also describes a nine-year retrospective examination of Air Force manpower requirements, funded authorizations, and assignments in key functional areas at representative installations. The objective of this research has been to develop policies and procedures to help the Air Force achieve and maintain an appropriate balance between funded manpower authorizations, skill levels, and PERSTEMPO.

The Air Force Directorate of Manpower and Organization (AF/A1M) sponsored this research, which was completed within the Manpower, Personnel, and Training Program of RAND Project AIR FORCE as part of a fiscal year 2005 project entitled "Comprehensive Requirements Determination Framework." This monograph is likely to be of interest to most people involved in human resource and human capital management.

Other related publications include the following:

- *Understrength Air Force Career Fields: A Force Management Approach*, Lionel A. Galway et al. (MG-131-AF). This monograph offers an overall framework for force management that would identify roles and organizations that could provide analysis and diagnosis of understrength conditions and could also execute appropriate policy interventions to solve these problems.

- *Differentiation in Military Human Resource Management*, Albert A. Robbert et al. (MR-838-OSD). This report describes and assesses the military human resource management system, identifies and evaluates alternatives to that system, recommends approaches for testing or implementing the most-promising alternatives (reduce weight of human capital development in promotions, reduce weight of occupational differences in promotions, increase special pay and bonuses, relax lateral-entry rules), and presents conclusions.
- *Analytic Architecture for Capabilities-Based Planning, Mission-System Analysis, and Transformation*, Paul Davis (MR-1513-OSD). This report puts capabilities-based planning in the larger context of defense activities generally, sketches an analytic architecture for carrying it out, and offers recommendations about how to proceed.

## RAND Project AIR FORCE

RAND Project AIR FORCE (PAF), a division of the RAND Corporation, is the U.S. Air Force's federally funded research and development center for studies and analyses. PAF provides the Air Force with independent analyses of policy alternatives affecting the development, employment, combat readiness, and support of current and future aerospace forces. Research is conducted in four programs: Aerospace Force Development; Manpower, Personnel, and Training; Resource Management; and Strategy and Doctrine.

Additional information about PAF is available on our Web site at http://www.rand.org/paf.

# Contents

# Figures

# Tables

# Summary

During the late 1990s and early 2000s, many U.S. Air Force organizations were finding that their manpower authorizations and the number of people assigned were inadequate to sustain both deployment and in-garrison missions with normal levels of military manpower availability. During deployments, nondeploying personnel assigned to many functional areas within the wings and commands were severely stressed and could not perform their normal home-base missions without working long hours. This problem stemmed in part from constrained military end strengths and other system constraints that restrict Air Force organizations from adequately adjusting military manpower and personnel levels to meet changing mission requirements. Moreover, both manning shortages and imbalances in skill levels further exacerbated the problem. To gain a greater understanding of the issues and policy implications, AF/A1M asked RAND PAF to undertake a detailed study and develop policy recommendations.

To execute this study, we

- collected historical manpower, personnel, and workload data and performed regression analyses to identify trends and patterns
- used Air Force manpower determinants, where available, to estimate manpower requirements for selected functions using planned workloads
- interviewed various Headquarters Air Force and major command manpower, personnel, and functional specialists

- performed historical analyses of selected wings, functional areas, and specialties to identify specific trends and patterns in generating requirements, funding authorizations, and assigning personnel.

This process led us to broaden our focus beyond manpower requirements to address the cumulative effect of the Air Force human resource system on wing-level manpower, skill levels, and PERSTEMPO.

The monograph's major findings are as follows:

- A comprehensive, systems-oriented human capital perspective is essential. Many of the issues identified during this study appear rooted in a lack of strategic direction compounded by fragmented approaches to human resource management. (See pp. 5–15.)
- The Air Force's process for determining manpower requirements needs resuscitation. The data in Chapters Three and Four raise serious questions about the adequacy of published manpower determinants, especially given the expeditionary nature of today's Air Force. (See pp. 19–61 and 66–69.)
- The Air Force needs one set of manpower books. Legacy computer systems resulted in the Air Force having at least three sets of manpower requirements. This contributed to discrepancies between the manpower authorized for wing-level missions and the actual number of people available. (See p. 78.)
- Skill-level imbalances affect productivity and contribute to workforce stress. If there are too many personnel in the lower three grades relative to the number of middle-grade trainers, the on-the-job training load can become a burden and can interfere with other mission activities. (See pp. 55–59.)
- Poor internal feedback between components of the human capital system impedes high system performance. During our interviews at both the Headquarters Air Force and major command levels, we found little evidence of feedback mechanisms between components of the human capital system. (See pp. 17–18.)

We recommend that the Air Force

- Implement an integrated manpower requirements architecture that considers workload, workforce sustainment, and workforce competencies. (See pp. 72–74.)
- Make greater use of dynamic simulation models to better understand the intersections of the manpower, personnel, and training subsystems. (See pp. 74–76.)
- Develop internal feedback loops between components of the human capital system that could be used to identify gaps in capabilities and/or misalignments between the manpower, personnel, and training activities. (See pp. 76–77.)
- Implement its Capability-Based Manpower Determination process as quickly as possible. (See pp. 77–78.)
- Field its Manpower Programming and Execution System as a means of eliminating multiple sets of books and explore ways to improve integration of MPES data into the personnel assignment and training systems. (See p. 78.)
- Establish and track metrics that compare planned against actual training burdens imposed on wing-level personnel. (See p. 79.)

# Acknowledgments

Our work could not have succeeded without the support and cooperation of the many representatives from the manpower, personnel, and functional communities. We are deeply indebted to Steve Sadler for providing us tremendous support in retrieving data from various manpower data systems. We are also indebted to Maj Dennis Miller and Lt Carsuelo Bampi for their support in providing personnel loading data. Capt David Ciesielski, Capt Jack Roberts, and William Scott shared data and insights that advanced our understanding of the management of various pipeline accounts. MSgt Susan Jaffery gave generously of her time to help us understand the Air Force PERSTEMPO data tracking system. The list of Headquarters Air Force and major command manpower, personnel, and functional representatives who met with us is extensive, and to all of them, we want to express our thanks. We would like to give a special thanks to Greg Parton, William Booth, and Brig Gen William Ard for their regular meetings and willingness to discuss the issues. Also, we thank RAND colleagues Ron Sortor and Albert Schroetel for their thoughtful reviews and critiques of our work. We thank other RAND colleagues, including Christine San, who made important contributions to the research.

# Abbreviations

| | |
|---|---|
| A1 | Deputy Chief of Staff for Personnel |
| A1M | Directorate of Manpower and Organization |
| A1P | Directorate of Force Management Policy |
| ACC | Air Combat Command |
| AETC | Air Education and Training Command |
| AEF | Air Expeditionary Force |
| AF | Air Force |
| AFB | Air Force base |
| AFI | Air Force instruction |
| AFMA | Air Force Manpower Agency |
| AFMC | Air Force Materiel Command |
| AFPC | Air Force Personnel Center |
| AFSC | Air Force Specialty Code |
| AFSOC | Air Force Special Operations Command |
| AFSPC | Air Force Space Command |
| AMC | Air Mobility Command |
| BMT | basic military training |
| CMS | capability-based manpower standards |
| CONOPS | concept of operations |

| | |
|---|---|
| CPG | career progression group |
| DAF | Department of the Air Force |
| DoD | Department of Defense |
| EAF | expeditionary aerospace force |
| EOD | explosive ordnance disposal |
| F&FP | Force and Financial Plan |
| FY | fiscal year |
| FYDP | Future Years Defense Program |
| GAO | Government Accountability Office |
| HAF MDS | Headquarters Air Force Manpower Data System |
| HQ USAF | Headquarters U.S. Air Force |
| LCOM | logistics composite model |
| MAJCOM | major command |
| MDS | Manpower Data System |
| MilPDS | Military Personnel Data System |
| MPES | Manpower Programming and Execution System |
| NCO | noncommissioned officer |
| OJT | on-the-job training |
| OPM | Office of Personnel Management |
| OSD | Office of the Secretary of Defense |
| PAF | Project AIR FORCE |
| PACAF | Pacific Air Forces |
| PERSTEMPO | personnel tempo |
| SAF/MR | Assistant Secretary of the Air Force for Manpower and Reserve Affairs |
| SORTS | Status of Resources and Training System |

| TDY | temporary duty |
| THRMIS | Human Resources Managers' Information System |
| TPR | trained personnel requirements |
| UMD | Unit Manpower Document |
| USAFE | U.S. Air Forces in Europe |
| USC | U.S. Code |
| UTC | unit type code |
| XPM | Manpower and Organization |
| YOS | years of service |

# CHAPTER ONE

# Introduction

This monograph examines the U.S. Air Force's military manpower, personnel, and training system in light of problems with personnel tempo (PERSTEMPO) among military personnel. It provides a description of the system and how it operates and a review of historical trends in manpower authorizations, manning levels, and workload.[1] The purpose of the study has been to identify potential policy changes needed to achieve and maintain an appropriate balance between manpower authorizations, skill levels, and PERSTEMPO. In this report, we provide five recommendations to help achieve and maintain that balance. The overarching recommendation is that a more-holistic approach to the human capital system with appropriate feedback loops can help the Air Force to align its human capital much more closely with its mission needs.

## Background

During the late 1990s and early 2000s, many Air Force organizations were finding that their manpower authorizations and the number of assigned people were not adequate to sustain both deployment and in-garrison missions with normal levels of military manpower availability. During deployments, nondeploying personnel assigned to many functional areas within the wings and commands were severely stressed and

---

[1]   The Air Force broadly defines PERSTEMPO as the time an individual spends away from home station.

could not perform their normal home-base missions without working well in excess of normal duty hours.

The stress the force experienced had several underlying causes. First, the Air Force had allowed its programmed force structure to exceed the capacity of its programmed end strength. Second, the manpower authorized to meet conventional peacetime needs may not be adequate for performing both normal installation missions and deployed missions. Third, even with adequate authorized spaces and full strength, there are not enough trained, skilled personnel in many specialties to fill higher-grade authorizations.

The Air Force has mounted two recent efforts to address this stress. Between April and July 2002, the Air Force conducted a large-scale review of active-duty and civilian positions to determine which positions directly contributed to its core competencies, with a view toward shifting military manpower resources away from requirements not associated with core competencies into critical, stressed career fields. As a follow-on to its Core Competency Review, the Air Force established the Human Capital Task Force in August 2002, giving it the tasks of focusing on implementing the resource shifts visualized in the Core Competency Review, developing other initiatives to help reduce personnel stress and solve the Air Force's critical manpower problems, and developing a comprehensive human capital plan to assist senior leaders in establishing and maintaining an appropriate long-term force under the expeditionary aerospace force (EAF) concept.

## Research Purpose and Scope

In this research, we studied the organization and operation of the military manpower, personnel, and training system of the Air Force in an attempt to understand how the system functions, where it might require improvement, and how it could be modified to function more effectively in dealing with current and future problems. To understand how these issues have affected the commands and their units, we also examined selected wings and functional areas (specialties) retrospectively, covering fiscal years (FYs) 1994 through 2002, using various statistical and data analysis tools. Through this analysis, we attempted to identify specific trends and patterns in generating requirements, funding authorizations, and assigning personnel.

Our objective was to develop recommendations for policies and procedures to help achieve and maintain a better balance between funded manpower authorizations, assignments, skill levels, and PERSTEMPO.

Most of the analyses reported here focus on management of enlisted personnel. However, the data systems, models, and management processes we describe generally either include officers or are parallel to similar structures for managing officers. Although our focus is on the enlisted force, our conclusions, we believe, apply to both officer and enlisted components of human capital management.

The Air Force's larger human capital management system must also consider nonmilitary labor pools: civil service employees, various non–civil-service categories of civilian employees, and contractors. Compared to management of military personnel, management of these components of the workforce is very decentralized. While we will occasionally refer to these components, particularly in discussing solutions to military human capital management problems, analyzing how they are managed was beyond the scope of this study.

## Methodology

We began by collecting historical manpower, personnel, and workload data and performing regression analyses to identify trends and patterns. We then used Air Force manpower determinants, when available, to calculate estimates for manpower requirements for selected functions using what would have been planned workloads. This allowed us to evaluate whether or not the observed trends and patterns correlated with apparent need.

We then broadened our focus beyond manpower requirements to address the cumulative effect of the Air Force human resource management system on wing-level manpower, skill levels, and PERSTEMPO.

These analyses led to five conclusions:

- A comprehensive, systems-oriented human capital perspective is essential. Many of the issues identified here appear rooted in the lack of strategic direction compounded by fragmented approaches to human capital management.
- The Air Force's process for determining manpower requirements needs resuscitation. Our analyses raise serious questions about the adequacy of published manpower determinants, especially given the expeditionary nature of today's Air Force.
- The Air Force needs one set of manpower books. It currently maintains at least three sets of manpower requirements. This contributed to discrepancies between the advertised number of people available for wing-level missions and the actual number available.
- Skill-level imbalances affect productivity and contribute to workforce stress. If there are too many personnel in the lower three grades relative to the number of trainers, the on-the-job training (OJT) load can become a burden and interfere with other mission activities.
- Poor internal feedback between components of the human capital management system impedes high system performance. During our interviews at both the Headquarters U.S. Air Force (HQ USAF) and MAJCOM levels, we found little evidence of feedback mechanisms between components of the system.

## Organization of This Monograph

In Chapter Two, we present a graphic description of the Air Force human capital management system. It presents a high-level view of this system and discusses the interactions between the components, how information moves through the system, and how system control theory might be used to improve how the system functions. Chapter Three discusses major Air Force–wide trends that result from the outputs of the subsystems described in Chapter Two. It demonstrates how the outputs of the system may be used as sensors and actuators.

In Chapter Four, we take a closer look at the trends in selected specialties at specific wings over the FY 1994 through FY 2002 period. More specifically, we examine how manpower requirements, funded authorizations, and assignments have changed during that time. This chapter also looks at the issues of skill mix within the specialties and the utility of existing manpower standards for requirement determination.

Chapter Five discusses ongoing changes in Air Force human capital systems and their implications. It also proposes additional initiatives and, in particular, looks at how these changes could address some of the issues raised in the previous chapters.

Chapter Six presents our conclusions and recommendations. Finally, the appendix describes manpower trends for a selection of specialties.

# CHAPTER TWO

# Air Force Manpower, Personnel, and Training System: An Ideal and an Overview

The knowledge, skills, abilities, and other competencies that comprise human capital are embodied in the Air Force's workforce. The Air Force's ability to capitalize on this critical asset is strongly influenced by its human resource management programs, practices, and policies. These, in turn, affect such important outcomes as how the Air Force accomplishes its goals, becomes more efficient, improves workforce commitment, and creates capacity for continual change.

In the Air Force, military human capital is managed within three well-defined *manpower*, *personnel*, and *training* subsystems. The manpower subsystem consists of the processes through which demand for human capital is defined and rationed; the personnel subsystem focuses on managing the supply of human capital; and the training subsystem focuses on development of human capital. Each subsystem has intricately related internal components and a nexus for transferring requisite data to the other subsystems. These subsystems are largely managed as individual stovepipes. As a consequence, few people have experience managing all three subsystems, and, concomitantly, little is known about the ways changes in one subsystem affect the others. Understanding each subsystem and its components is necessary but insufficient to explain the health of the overall human capital management system. Without knowledge of the related functions and their interactions, major positive contributions from one subsystem may be negated by deficiencies in others.

In this chapter, we describe the benefits and characteristics of a comprehensive, well-integrated system of systems for managing the

Air Force's human capital. We then synoptically describe the current manpower, personnel, and training subsystems used to develop and control the content of the Air Force's enlisted manpower force. Since our research focuses on manpower requirements, we explore the three subsystems from a manpower perspective, seeking to understand where greater integration of the three subsystems could improve the manpower requirements process.

## The Ideal: An Integrated System of Systems

A comprehensive, well-integrated system of systems might yield three potential benefits: a leveraging of interactions, a clarifying and synchronizing of roles, and better strategic alignment of human resource to organizational needs.

### Leveraged Interactions

The various human capital subsystems interact with other systems, such as the Planning, Programming, and Budgeting System and Air Expeditionary Force (AEF) planning and deployment systems, at many different points, and multiple human resource components may intersect these systems at the same point. Adopting a broader, systems-oriented perspective should yield efficiencies by strengthening value-added intersections while eliminating efforts that are duplicative, ineffective, or irrelevant.

Also, leveraging information technology could provide a common suite of tools across human resource stovepipes and the various functional communities for collecting and using data and information. A common suite of tools would contribute to consistency in terminology and accounting of resources, facilitate configuration control and data dissemination, and simplify training for career-field managers. Further, existing information technology allows data to reside in a single repository, in which each data element exists only once, regardless of how many processes it serves. Lastly, the power of Web-based technology enables greater consolidation of data-intensive operations and, simultaneously, increases the Air Force–wide dissemination of appropriate human resource management information to career-field managers and decisionmakers.

## Clarifying and Synchronizing Roles

Capitalizing on synergy and leveraging information technology across human resource components and the functional communities should streamline processes and, thereby, offer potential to shorten the time from a strategy's conception to its execution. Concomitant with streamlining processes should be clarification of roles and synchronization of the human capital components (traditional ones and those embedded in functional communities). Three areas are of particular concern. One is a *controller*—a mechanism that provides direction, measures progress, and calibrates inputs based on feedback. The trends discussed in Chapters Three and Four suggest that this role is not adequately performed. In this context, the human resource controller—the Assistant Secretary of the Air Force for Manpower and Reserve Affairs (SAF/MR) and the Air Force Deputy Chief of Staff for Personnel (AF/A1)[1]— would set the direction for Air Force–wide human resource strategies, lead implementation of Air Force–wide human capital plans, and oversee progress. Armed with appropriate models and tools, SAF/MR and AF/A1 would continually scan the environment, identifying and analyzing external and internal human capital opportunities and threats that may be crucial to Air Force success. They would establish clear strategic visions and serve as directional beacons defining which opportunities should be explored and which should be avoided. The objective is to ensure greater strategic control and increased consistency across functional communities and major commands (MAJCOMs).

Another area relates to the roles of human resource specialists and career-field managers. Many human resource activities, such as leading efforts to define requirements and training needs, are performed by career-field managers. Clarifying and synchronizing these roles, responsibilities, relationships, and areas of contribution would help establish expectations and accountability. Many back-office tasks, such

---

[1]    These were the office symbols at the time of publication.

as data collection and analysis, could be consolidated and performed by specialists, freeing career-field managers to devote more time to resolving the underlying strategic and operational issues. Given the right training, tools, and resource flexibilities, human resource specialists could work with the functional communities and commanders to develop comprehensive strategies to shape the workforce and meet Air Force goals.

A third area relates to human capital stewardship. Lengnick-Hall and Lengnick-Hall (2002, p. 33) observed that the "role of human capital steward requires accumulating, concentrating, conserving, complementing, and recovering the collective knowledge, skills, and abilities within an organization." They stressed that stewardship implies guiding the organization without dominating it. To perform this role effectively, human resource managers would need macro-level models and tools to provide information on how, when, and where to buy, build, borrow, bounce, or bind human resources (Ulrich, 1999, pp. 126–138).

### Better Strategic Alignment

Several studies underscore that, for human resources legitimately to be considered a strategic asset, the human resource architecture should be aligned with the organization's mission, goals, and objectives and integrated into the organization's strategic plans, performance plans, and budgets.[2] Strategic alignment is a balancing act that involves setting a direction, linking processes and systems, and making the adjustments

---

[2]    Strategic alignment is one of the five key dimensions of human capital management for the federal government's Office of Personnel Management (OPM). The OPM framework (see OPM, 2006) was developed in collaboration with human resource directors from federal agencies and drew heavily on private-sector practices. The Government Accountability Office (GAO) has integration and alignment (under Strategic Human Capital Planning) as one of its eight critical success factors (GAO, 2002). Becker, Ulrich, and Huselid (2001) collected data on human resource management quality from nearly 3,000 firms and followed the firms' performance over time. They concluded that firms with more-effective human resource management systems consistently outperformed their peers. They argue that high-performance organizations view human resources as a system embedded in the larger system of the firm's strategy implementation. These firms manage and measure the relationship between these systems and the firm's performance.

needed to achieve the organization's current and future missions in a dynamic environment.

The alignment occurs in two dimensions. Horizontal alignment, from a human capital perspective, suggests that human resource professionals are working in concert with senior leaders and managers to develop, implement, and assess the human capital policies and procedures needed to achieve the organization's shared vision and most important objectives.[3] Vertical alignment is about rapidly and effectively deploying the human capital strategy throughout the organization.[4] Vertical alignment suggests the people understand organization-wide goals and how their roles, systems, and processes contribute to achieving the mission and objectives. Achieving strategic alignment implies that all activities are connected in a manner that allows them to complement each other and contribute to achieving the organization's overarching mission, goals, and objectives.

Strategic alignment argues for a top-down perspective that steers human capital management. Absent a top-down perspective to provide focus and consistency, there are likely to be a multitude of conflicting decisions and policies. As we will illustrate, the Air Force's approach to human capital management has, de facto, been more of a middle- to bottom-up approach focused on groups of work centers and functions and on collections of specialties with limited corporate perspective across functions and specialties. This contributes to a stovepipe view of the workforce and inhibits the Air Force's ability to align human resources to best achieve strategic goals and objectives. Poorly aligned human capital components, like cars out of alignment, are hard to steer and do not respond well to changes in direction. Misaligned components can result in wasteful and counterproductive activities, as well as the expenditure of unnecessary energy and resources. As Robbert et al. (1997) noted, strategically aligned human capital management systems have three important attributes. First, the organization's overarching

---

[3]    In OPM (2006), the human resource *collaboration* critical success factor would be equivalent to horizontal alignment.

[4]    In OPM (2006), the human capital *focus* critical success factor would be equivalent to vertical alignment.

strategies inform decisions about required workforce characteristics and behaviors. Second, desired workforce characteristics and behaviors inform strategic choices made in designing broad human capital policies, practices, and procedures. Last, these design choices shape specific human capital policies, practices, and procedures.

Adopting a comprehensive, well-integrated system-of-systems approach should allow the Air Force to address more fully such critical questions as the following: (1) Are its human capital strategies aligned with current and future missions, goals, and objectives? (2) What is the actual human capital cost of its current and future missions? (3) What changes in human capital policies, programs, and practices would yield the greatest contributions to the Air Force and national security? This broader perspective should result in a more-explicit understanding of how the various types of human resources contribute to the Air Force's mission and how best to allocate the resources among competing demands. This systems-oriented perspective should yield a better understanding of how the human capital components work together to produce a workforce that meets the current and future needs of the Air Force.

## The Current Subsystems

In our view, the degree of integration of the three subsystems is far from ideal. Processes in the manpower subsystem strongly influence processes in the personnel subsystem, which in turn strongly influence processes in the training subsystem, but feedback loops from the downstream processes to the upstream processes are weak. As a result, the upstream processes may drive toward objectives that are infeasible, excessively costly, or otherwise inconsistent with overall Air Force objectives.

### The Manpower Subsystem

The manpower subsystem is primarily concerned with identifying the jobs and associated requirements needed to perform assigned missions. The manpower components ascertain these requirements and distribute manpower authorizations for accomplishing missions effectively and economically within organizational and resource constraints. Within the Air Staff, the Directorate of Manpower and Organization (AF/A1M) and the managers of other functions, in partnership with the Air Force Manpower Agency (AFMA), provide tools that can help determine required numbers and skill mixes of personnel (Department of the Air Force [DAF], 2003d). Collectively, the Air Force prioritizes these *requirements* and chooses a subset that fits within its allocated aggregate manpower budget. Requirements within these "funded" subsets are commonly called *manpower authorizations*. Theoretically, the cumulative manpower requirements should represent what the Air Force believes it needs for its programmed force structure and capabilities. In contrast, the cumulative manpower authorizations should represent what the Air Force has been able to fund, given fiscal and end-strength constraints.

The funded manpower authorizations should conform to the Department of Defense (DoD) Future Years Defense Program (FYDP), which should in turn conform to congressionally approved end-strength limits. DoD uses program element codes in the FYDP to budget for and control its resources, including manpower. The Air Force uses its Force and Financial Plan (F&FP) to budget for and control its portion of the DoD program element codes. AF/A1M then bases its allocation of manpower resources to the commands for execution of approved programs on the F&FP. The commands translate the allocation into manpower authorizations by updating unit manpower documents (UMDs) with organization, Air Force Specialty Code (AFSC), grade, program element, etc. Local manpower offices provide these UMDs to local commanders, and periodically (usually monthly), the Air Force Personnel Center (AFPC) receives an electronic file of all manpower authorizations.

Figure 2.1 depicts the interaction of the manpower, personnel, and training subsystems within the overall Air Force military human capital management system. The specific elements depicted here are peculiar to management of the enlisted force. In most cases, similar elements exist for managing the officer force.[5] As shown in Figure 2.1, the manpower subsystem has two important linkages with the other human capital subsystems. The one most visible is the UMD. The UMD identifies the jobs that the personnel subsystem targets in distributing people to meet the Air Force's overall needs. The other linkage, future specialties and skill projection, is less visible but is critical to defining future recruiting and training needs. Once a year, AF/A1M provides the Directorate of Force Management Policy (AF/A1P) a three-year projection of needed enlisted specialties and skills, given projected force-structure changes. These skill projections start the trained personnel requirements (TPR) process, which seeks to ensure sufficient numbers of trained people in each specialty.

Figure 2.1 suggests that a useful metric within the manpower subsystem would be the trend in funded enlisted authorizations versus total enlisted requirements. This metric is employed in subsequent sections to illustrate its potential utility as a warning sign of work center stress and the need for process reengineering.

### The Personnel Subsystem

The personnel subsystem is primarily concerned with providing mission-ready people to unit commanders. The composition of the enlisted force is controlled through various policies and programs relating to procurement, classification, development, promotion, separation, and retirement. The distribution of enlisted personnel is based on operational, rotational, and training requirements. The composition and distribution of the enlisted force determine which people are matched against funded manpower authorizations to execute unit missions.

The Air Force uses a centralized assignment process to distribute people in accordance with unit needs, ensure compliance with laws and directives, and ensure assignments are equitable and cost-effective (DAF, 2003b). As Figure 2.1 indicates, AF/A1 develops Air Force poli-

---

[5]   For illustrative purposes, the differences are minor. For example, officers commissioned via the Air Force Academy do not receive their basic military training (BMT) via the Air Education and Training Command (AETC). However, we restricted the scope of the research to the enlisted force.

Figure 2.1
The Human Capital Management System of the Air Force

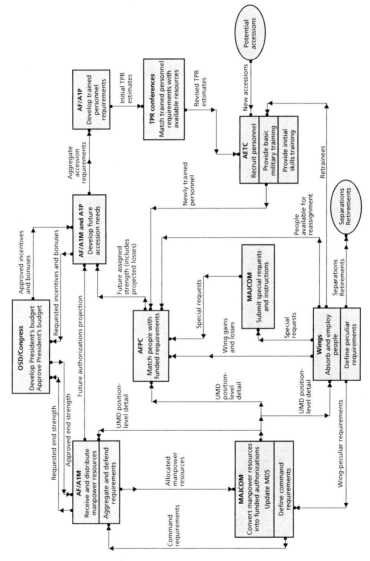

cies and guidance for personnel assignments. Using these policies and guidance for most enlisted assignments, AFPC projects losses and rotations from each unit, compares the strength after losses to manpower requirements, and determines required backfills.[6] AFPC seeks to come as close as possible to providing commanders with the right number of skilled people and in the proper grades and specialties to perform their missions. Funded authorizations often exceed the number of people available; therefore, AFPC seeks to distribute people as equitably as possible among the MAJCOMs and units with a specialty and grade according to the manning unit group,[7] plug table,[8] and manning priority plans. As Figure 2.1 suggests, AFPC is the center of activity for matching enlisted people with vacant positions.

A useful metric for how well the human capital system is performing is the degree to which the people match the funded authorizations. These data are widely tracked among the personnel components of the human capital system; however, we found little cross-flow of these data between the personnel and manpower components. During our interviews with manpower and personnel representatives, several anecdotal examples were given that suggested that, when trends in a specialty are consistently below a given threshold, this information would be useful in accessing workforce stress and, perhaps, signaling the need to reengineer processes or use alternative labor sources.[9]

---

[6]  The Air Force Senior Leader Management Office, rather than AFPC, manages assignment of chief master sergeants.

[7]  Units are grouped by type for manning and statistical analysis.

[8]  MAJCOMs (or equivalents) may use the plug table, a computer program maintained by AFPC, to control some features of the allocations they receive by inserting values for special experience identifier, personnel processing code, security access, and other variables.

[9]  In fall 2002, the Air Force developed a stress formula giving consideration to the number of manpower authorizations, manning level, and number of deployments. This formula is used to guide the redistribution of manpower authorizations from nonstressed to stressed specialties. However, this information has not been integrated into the requirement determination process to influence reengineering and use of technology and alternative labor sources.

## The Training Subsystem

The training subsystem is primarily concerned with equipping people with the right skills and capabilities to meet mission requirements. While military training programs are structured for career-long learning, our analysis addresses only enlisted initial skill training. Broadly, two kinds of training requirements exist: quantitative and qualitative. The quantitative requirements, addressed in this report, are derived through the TPR process. Budget decisions, legislative appropriations and authorizations, manpower processes, and personnel losses and cross-flows drive the quantitative requirements. The qualitative requirements relate to course content and are driven by career-field managers via utilization and training workshops. The qualitative requirements are not addressed in this report.

The Air Force uses the TPR process to allocate enlisted accessions and cross-flows (retrainees) for training. As Figure 2.1 shows, AF/A1M provides AF/A1P a three-year projection of future manpower authorizations by specialty, skill level, grade, and FY. This represents the expected future demand adjusted for projected force-structure changes, mission changes, etc. Likewise, the AF/A1P, with data from AFPC, develops a projection of the future inventory (current inventory adjusted for expected losses and promotions by FY). This represents the expected future supply. The expected future demand is compared to the expected future supply, and the differences provide initial estimates of TPR for the current plus three FYs. These estimates are reconciled to expected aggregate accessions and cross-flows. TPR managers prepare preliminary TPRs and coordinate them through the appropriate functional resource managers for review and adjustment (DAF, 1993b). After the reviews and an October or November TPR conference (also called the training flow management conference), the TPRs are finalized and provided to appropriate training managers to schedule accessions and training for future FYs.

AETC uses the TPR to construct the portion of the Programmed Technical Training that pertains to Air Force students flowing through initial skill training. This three-year training plan reflects expected class dates and expected class sizes.

As Figure 2.1 suggests, AETC is the nucleus for training activities. Its mission is "recruiting, training, and educating professional airmen to sustain the combat capability of America's Air Force" (AETC, 2002a, p. 3). Thus, AETC is the pipeline for replenishing the Air Force's enlisted force. During FY 2002, for example, AETC recruited nearly 38,000 people for active-duty enlisted positions; graduated more than 43,000 from BMT;[10] and graduated 110,000 people from resident technical training courses (AETC, 2002b). AETC's student output has a direct effect on the number of people with the right skills and capabilities to meet mission requirements. As one example, if AETC cannot recruit sufficient people with the appropriate aptitude indexes, the numbers graduating from BMT will be insufficient to fill the specified seats for technical training. If the requisite technical training seats are not filled, the number of graduates will not meet the requirements TPR specifies, and unit manning shortages will normally occur.

The training components capture several metrics relating to training production (DAF, 2004b). AF/A1P groups and tracks specialties based on the degree to which their published TPR would sustain them at, above, or below 100 percent. AETC Technical Training produces a quarterly report of pipeline training requirements execution and, when necessary with appropriate coordination, may adjust the number of seats allocated for training. The Air Force Recruiting Service maintains metrics on the quality, aptitude, quantity, and timing of recruits. These are just a few of the metrics retained within various training components whose trends could prove beneficial to other subsystems within the Air Force human capital management system.

## An Incomplete System: Inadequate Feedback Between Subsystems

The Air Force's human capital management system is complex, involving myriad units, people, processes, and behaviors (Armstrong and Moore, 1980).[11] Traditional analyses divide the system into its sub-

---

[10] The 43,000 BMT graduates include those completing BMT for entry into reserve and guard units.

[11] Although published in 1980, Armstrong and Moore still provide one of the most comprehensive descriptions of the various roles and their interactions.

systems and focus on the individual pieces. These analyses can provide insights into specific components of each subsystem (Hosek, et al., 2004; Ausink, Cave, and Carrillo, 2003). However, the components alone cannot do what the system does. Although the subsystems may operate with varying degrees of independence, any major change in one area ripples through the larger system. To maintain the appropriate equilibrium between manpower, skill levels, and PERSTEMPO, the subsystems must efficiently communicate and collectively adapt to the internal and external environment surrounding human capital issues.

A more-holistic approach to managing enlisted human capital would take into account larger numbers of interactions between system components.[12] Seeing the bigger picture may lead to strikingly different conclusions and new solution possibilities. For example, if the manpower component receives feedback that the accessions and training components will not be able to satisfactorily meet the requirements in a particular specialty for several years, it could trigger consideration of alternative labor sources or capital-labor substitution. Likewise, if the manpower component receives feedback that the required grade distribution is not attainable, it could trigger consideration of alternative grade mixes and workforce sizes to achieve the same productivity envisaged in the original grade mix and workforce size requirements.

The principle of feedback is what makes systems perform as intended. In practical terms, the feedback loop returns information about the difference between actual and specified results to the controlling source regarding an action, event, or process so that evaluative or corrective actions may be taken. A critical aspect of control system design is determining the performance specifications and what types of sensors and actuators will be used (Doyle, Francis, and Tannenbaum, 1990). It is important to realize that, inevitably, real-world dynamics will produce uncertainty, limiting the achievable benefits of feedback. Nonetheless, in the next two chapters, we examine historical trends in manpower, personnel, and training data to identify potential feedback sensors in an effort to achieve and maintain equilibrium.

---

[12]  See Galway et al. (2005) for a discussion of operational and strategic challenges relating to a more-holistic approach for officer resources.

# CHAPTER THREE

# Major Air Force–Wide Trends

This section reviews Air Force–wide data for FYs 1994 through 2002 to identify several prominent trends and their associated consequences. Through this review, we demonstrate that significant data are collected and readily available. Our field interviews, conducted from September 2003 through February 2004 at HQ USAF, two MAJCOMs, AFMA, and AFPC, confirmed that abundant data were being collected and, indeed, that metrics were being monitored within each of the respective human capital management stovepipes. However, our data collection and interviews found little evidence that metrics were being shared between the stovepipes. After reviewing the trends, we conclude this chapter by suggesting that, if the right metrics were routinely collected and disseminated across the human capital management system, they could serve as sensors to warn of unfavorable trends and provide feedback to help identify force-shaping options.

## Unachievable Expectations

Given existing constraints and fiscal realities, UMDs appear to have made promises that the rest of the human capital management system could not fulfill. UMDs are extracts from the manpower data system that document, including specialty and grade, the military and civilian positions each organization is authorized. To unit commanders and supervisors, manpower authorizations represent the number of people they should expect to perform the mission. Several dynamics in the system often make providing that number of people infeasible.

## Authorizations Sometimes Exceed End Strength

Congress, in the annual National Defense Authorization Act, mandates military personnel strengths for each service. These strength levels are based on the services' requests via the President's Budget and congressional hearings and deliberations. Originally a personnel strength ceiling, the active-duty strength levels have become a de facto ceiling and floor (10 USC 115 and 10 USC 691) and must be attained within a specified tolerance by the end of each FY.[1] The strength levels encompass all active military personnel who are paid from congressionally appropriated funds and programmed in the FYDP. For FY 1994, the Air Force's enlisted strength was set at 341,300.[2] That year was part of a downward trend that continued until FY 2001, when mandated enlisted strength dropped to 280,410. Merely comparing the Air Force's documented requirements and military personnel counts with approved strength levels provides potential feedback sensors for the human capital system.

Figure 3.1 compares the cumulative enlisted funded requirements, commonly called manpower authorizations,[3] to mandated end-strength levels for FY 1994 through 2002. Each column is the sum of manpower authorizations in force-structure and pipeline accounts.[4] The

---

[1]   The National Defense Authorization Act for FY 2004 added end-of-quarter strength reporting requirements.

[2]   Subtracting congressionally approved commissioned officer strength levels from total active-duty strength levels derives enlisted strength levels.

[3]   Requirements are documented in UMDs as being either funded or unfunded. Funded requirements are commonly called *manpower authorizations* and serve as the basis for manning entitlements. Unfunded requirements are positions identified as necessary to accomplish the unit's mission; however, funding is not available, and they are not included in the calculation of manning entitlements.

[4]   *Force-structure manpower authorizations* are documented as funded in the UMDs and reflect organization, AFSC, grade, program element, etc. Force-structure authorizations are also called *permanent party authorizations*. Local commanders and supervisors expect these authorizations to be filled with people. *Pipeline accounts*, also called *individuals accounts* or *students, transients, prisoners, and patients accounts*, are centrally managed manpower authorizations for people in transient, holding (prisoners, patients, and separatees), and student status. Typically, these accounts contain total manpower counts but do not reflect organization, AFSC, and grade.

black horizontal line represents 100 percent of the mandated enlisted strength. Starting in 1997, aggregate enlisted authorizations exceeded enlisted strength levels. Because the actual number of enlisted people is capped at approved end-strength levels, 100-percent manning was not possible during the late 1990s without violating the ceilings.

## Out-of-Balance Manpower Books

Two primary reasons for the imbalances shown in Figure 3.1 were unimplemented manpower reductions and overallocations. For example, the Air Force was levied reductions that were targeted for management headquarters and competitive sourcing activities that were not fully distributed to the commands.[5] These unimplemented reductions contributed to the commands' accounts being greater than the end strength reflected in the FYDP. As another example, programmed mission and/or equipment changes do not always occur as planned.[6] These deviations may cause the commands to overallocate manpower authorizations to match mission changes because the normal programming cycle would be unable to respond. These overallocations do not produce additional people; they create personnel shortages that are distributed across the Air Force.

To diminish these problems, the Air Force implemented a balance-the-books effort in 2003. The ultimate goal was to have the sum of the UMDs equal the FYDP and to keep the books balanced by working through manpower allocations. The effort had several tenets. First, keep the manpower connected to program content. If program changes warrant an increase in manpower authorizations and if the end strength or dollars are not available, the program changes should

---

[5]   The FY 2000 National Defense Authorization Act directed DoD to reduce the number of personnel in management headquarters by 15 percent by FY 2002. At end of 2002, the Air Force still needed to implement a 7.5-percent reduction. During the late 1990s, a portion of anticipated savings (dollars and end strength) was reprogrammed from operation and maintenance accounts to modernization accounts. For a variety of reasons, the services were not able to reach the targeted end-strength reductions. See GAO (2001).

[6]   Phasing aircraft in or out, such as the C-9 Nightingale retirement, and transferring missions between commands are examples.

**Figure 3.1**
**Manpower Authorizations as Percentage of Enlisted Strength**

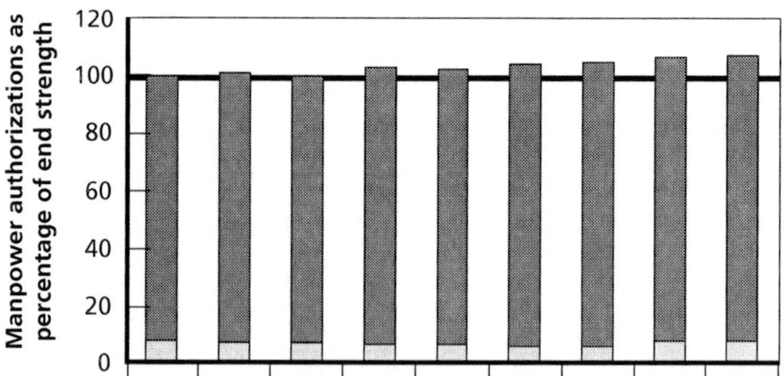

| FY: | 1994 | 1995 | 1996 | 1997 | 1998 | 1999 | 2000 | 2001 | 2002 |
|---|---|---|---|---|---|---|---|---|---|
| ■ End strength (000s) | 341.3 | 317.9 | 308.6 | 299.4 | 294.6 | 286.2 | 284.3 | 283.8 | 284.7 |
| ▨ Force structure athoriations (000s) | 313.0 | 296.5 | 283.7 | 286.9 | 279.3 | 280.0 | 277.8 | 275.5 | 282.3 |
| ☐ Pipeline athoriations | 24.8 | 20.9 | 20.7 | 18.9 | 19.2 | 15.7 | 16.8 | 21.1 | 20.4 |

SOURCE: Data adapted from Air Force Manpower Data Systems.
RAND MG492-3.1

be disapproved or offsets identified. Second, commands must submit a balanced program objectives memorandum, including manpower authorizations. Third, manpower bills and savings from Air Force–directed changes would be paid by the commands or returned to the corporate Air Force. Fourth, manpower changes that the Office of the Secretary of Defense (OSD) has directed, including reductions, would be implemented and not deferred.

## Personnel Strength Typically Equals or Exceeds End Strength

Figure 3.2 compares the number of enlisted people on active duty at the end of the FY to the mandated end-strength levels. Each column is the sum of enlisted people in the force-structure and pipeline accounts. To achieve end-strength levels, personnel gains and losses must be managed closely. Figure 3.2 shows the Air Force was reasonably close to end-strength targets for all years except 2002. For 2001, the Air Force was 3,400 people short of end strength, about 1.1 percent. For 2002, the Air Force ended the year 9,000 over end strength, largely because of a stop-loss implemented in October 2001 to support Operations Enduring Freedom and Noble Eagle. In years when the number of people matched end strength, simply comparing Figures 3.1 and 3.2 would imply units were undermanned by the difference between the cumulative manpower authorizations and the mandated end-strength levels. For example, the Air Force documented 294,558 manpower authorizations but an end strength of 284,311 in 2000. This suggests, in the aggregate, that force-structure units would have been short 10,247 people (3.5 percent). However, as the following discussion of the pipeline accounts indicates, this calculation understates the problem.

## Pipeline Accounts

People in pipeline accounts are in transient, holding (patients, prisoners, separatees), or student status and are not available for duty in force-structure units. These accounts are necessary to renew, develop, and sustain the force.

**Figure 3.2**
**Enlisted Personnel as Percentage of End Strength**

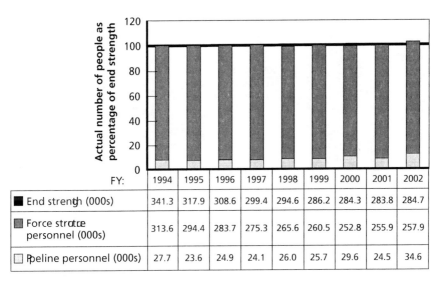

| FY: | 1994 | 1995 | 1996 | 1997 | 1998 | 1999 | 2000 | 2001 | 2002 |
|---|---|---|---|---|---|---|---|---|---|
| ■ End strength (000s) | 341.3 | 317.9 | 308.6 | 299.4 | 294.6 | 286.2 | 284.3 | 283.8 | 284.7 |
| ▨ Force structure personnel (000s) | 313.6 | 294.4 | 283.7 | 275.3 | 265.6 | 260.5 | 252.8 | 255.9 | 257.9 |
| ▢ Pipeline personnel (000s) | 27.7 | 23.6 | 24.9 | 24.1 | 26.0 | 25.7 | 29.6 | 24.5 | 34.6 |

SOURCE: Data adapted from Air Force Personnel Data Systems.
RAND MG492-3.2

All active-duty people are counted in either a force-structure or a pipeline account. Normally, the total people in these accounts cannot exceed congressionally authorized strength levels. Thus, if the actual number of people in pipeline accounts is greater than the programmed number, force-structure manning will normally suffer accordingly.

Data in Figure 3.3 indicate the actual enlisted pipeline was consistently greater than the programmed pipeline. The smallest difference was nearly 2,700 in FY 1994. The largest difference was over 14,000 in FY 2002. These data would suggest that 1 to 5 percent of the enlisted personnel shortages absorbed by force-structure units could be attributed to these systemic differences. These shortages must be added to the shortages depicted in Figure 3.1 to determine the net shortages in the force structure. Unit-level data entry problems (mischaracterizing individuals as students, patients, prisoners, or permanent parties) make the magnitude of the differences debatable; nonetheless, the potential effects on unit manning warrant additional senior management attention to minimize the differences and improve data accuracy.

**Figure 3.3**
**Size of Pipeline Accounts (Programmed Manpower Authorizations versus Actual Number of Enlisted Personnel)**

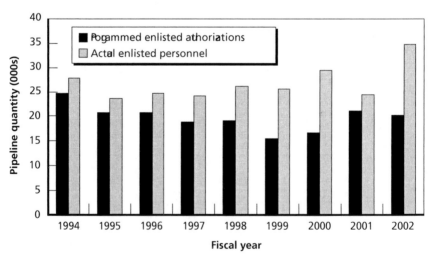

SOURCE: Data adapted from Air Force Manpower and Personnel Data Systems.
RAND MG492-3.3

Minimizing the programmed versus actual difference is complicated by the difference between goals and reality. The actual enlisted pipeline size is strongly influenced by each year's non–prior service accessions. Accessions are driven by future needs and retention rates. The programmed pipeline size is estimated at least two years in advance, using projected needs and targeted goals for retention. Normally, retention goals are around 55 percent for first-term enlisted members, 75 percent for second-term members, and 95 percent for members with more than ten years of service (YOS). The actual pipeline is based on future needs and nearer-term forecasts of retention rates. From 1997 through 2000, Air Force actual retention rates did not reach these goals (DAF, 2002a, p. 46), resulting in the need for more accessions to meet end-strength levels. Increased accessions led to more students and transients, causing the actual pipeline accounts to be larger than what was programmed in the defense plans. These larger-than-planned pipeline accounts occur at the expense of force-structure units.

**Effects of Imbalances**

When the total number of manpower authorizations consistently exceeds congressionally approved personnel strength levels, unachievable expectations are created about combat capability and manning levels. The Air Force uses unit type codes (UTCs) to predefine groupings of equipment and/or manpower to provide specific combat capabilities. The stated goal is to posture as many manpower authorizations into UTCs as possible (DAF, 2002b). When the number of manpower authorizations in the UTCs exceeds the number of people, the unit's actual combat capability is overstated. Similarly, the Air Force uses the UMD to indicate how many people should be required to perform the mission. If a position is shown as funded, commanders and supervisors expect that a person will be available to fill it and that a vacancy is temporary. Because local commanders and supervisors are not privy to the larger picture, they would not realize that the dynamics of strength levels, pipeline planning, imbalanced manpower books, and fiscal realities have made 100-percent unit manning unachievable for most units.

Cost estimates associated with such initiatives as competitive sourcing and base closures are also affected by manpower imbalances. These initiatives use UMDs as part of their cost baselines. If the baselines for these analyses are not accurate, the projected savings or costs will be inaccurate as well.

## Authorizations and People Are Less Than Required

The UMD distinguishes between manpower authorizations (funded requirements) and unfunded requirements. Air Force policy is to quantify total manpower needs by documenting both funded and unfunded manpower requirements (DAF, 2003d). Unfunded requirements are validated positions necessary to accomplish a unit's mission but deferred because of budgetary and/or end-strength constraints. As stated in AFI 38-201, *Determining Manpower Requirements*, valid unfunded requirements may stem from (1) application of approved manpower determinants, such as manpower standards; (2) the logistics composite model (LCOM); (3) aircrew ratios for authorized primary aircraft inventory; and (4) program objective memorandum and budget estimate tab P initiatives (DAF, 2003d, p. 20).[7] Although these requirements are validated as necessary to accomplish the mission, they are not included in the unit's personnel entitlements because there is no funding. The targets for the personnel and training subsystems are derived from funded requirements, not the total requirements. Unfunded requirements receive no visibility in the training and personnel components of the human capital management system.

Figure 3.4 shows that the numbers of enlisted authorizations and personnel have been consistently less than total requirements. In the aggregate, authorizations averaged 97.1 percent of enlisted requirements, with a span of 96.3 to 97.8 percent. Similarly, the aggregate number of enlisted personnel, averaged 95.2 percent of requirements, ranging from 92.4 to 98.5 percent. Authorizations constantly hovered

---

[7]   Budget estimate tab P contains procurement initiatives.

**Figure 3.4**
**Comparison of Total Enlisted Requirements, Manpower Authorizations,**
**and Personnel**

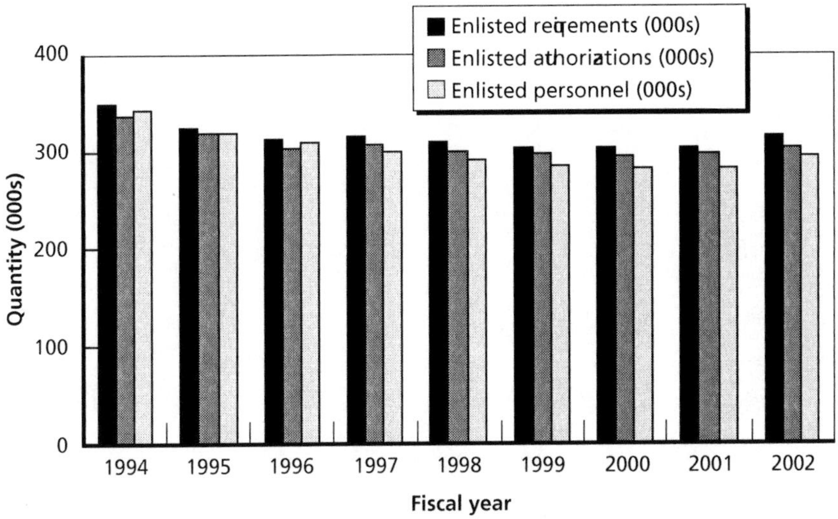

SOURCE: Data adapted from Air Force Manpower and Personnel Data Systems.
RAND *MG492-3.4*

around 97 percent of requirements while the personnel percentage was at 98 percent during the drawdown years, before declining to 92.4 percent by 2001 and rising back to 93.0 percent in 2002. These aggregate numbers include authorizations and personnel in the pipeline account; thus, the percentages in reality overstate the availability of people to meet the requirements.

**Shortages Were Not Evenly Distributed**

The above data suggest, given then-existing methods of operation, distribution of bases and equipment, and manpower mix (the major variables influencing total manpower requirements), that the Air Force was short of enlisted personnel before the additional demands precipitated by the events of September 11, 2001. Further, Figures 3.5 and 3.6 indicate that the personnel shortages were not distributed evenly across

**Figure 3.5**
**Comparison of Enlisted Requirements, Authorizations, and Personnel for Operations and Maintenance Specialties (1- and 2-series)**

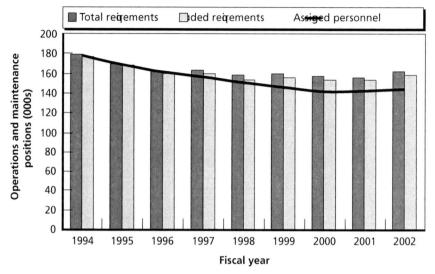

SOURCE: Data adapted from Air Force Manpower and Personnel Data Systems.
RAND *MG492-3.5*

specialties. Figure 3.5 shows the manpower authorization shortage in operations (1-series) and maintenance (2-series) specialties. During the drawdown years, the assigned personnel strength often exceeded manpower authorizations and averaged 99.5 percent of total requirements. After the drawdown, the assigned strength averaged 92.0 percent of total requirements, with the shortages ranging from 6,900 people in 1997 to 18,800 in 2002. Figure 3.6 shows the relative shortages were greater in support specialties (3-series). During the drawdown, the number of assigned personnel was nearly equal to the manpower authorizations and averaged 96 percent of total requirements. After the drawdown, the assigned strength averaged 88 percent of total requirements, with the shortage averaging 10,600 people.

If the requirements are accurate, these shortages suggest that commanders and supervisors would have had difficulties performing missions requiring enlisted crewmembers, weapon system maintain-

**Figure 3.6**
**Comparison of Enlisted Requirements, Authorizations, and Personnel for Support Specialties (3-series)**

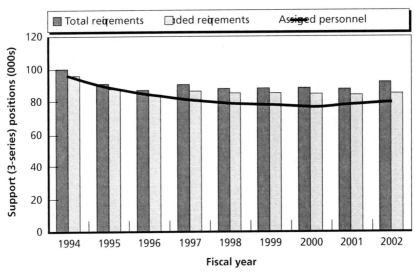

SOURCE: Data adapted from Air Force Manpower and Personnel Data Systems.
RAND *MG492-3.6*

ers, and various support specialists. Additionally, the magnitude of the difficulties would have varied by specialty. In Chapter Four and the appendix, we examine several specific specialties in greater detail and will argue that requirements were often understated rather than accurate.

## Unit-Level Effects

Operational readiness is the ability of units to deliver their planned outputs without unacceptable delay (DAF, 1997a). The status of each operational unit's personnel is continuously monitored and reported in the Status of Resources and Training System (SORTS) (DAF, 2003c). SORTS indicates the level of selected resources and training required to undertake the mission(s) for which a unit is organized or designed. Typically, the unit's manpower authorizations in the UMD serve as the baseline for measuring and reporting personnel status. For units that only have deployment missions, UTCs serve as the baseline. Units are considered P-1 if their assigned personnel strength is from 90 to 100 percent of the manpower authorizations. A rating of P-1 indicates the unit possesses the required people to undertake all missions assigned. Units are considered P-4 if they are at 69 percent or less, which indicates that additional people are required for a unit to undertake its currently assigned missions. Ratings of P-2 or P-3 indicate degrees of readiness degradation.

Figure 3.7 provides a different perspective on the readiness issues by considering total requirements. For this analysis, pipeline accounts were removed from the data, leaving the requirements, authorizations, and permanent party personnel actually in the units. Manpower authorizations as a percentage of total requirements followed the previous trends, averaging 97 percent. Recall that unfunded requirements are not visible to the personnel assignment components; nonetheless, the

**Figure 3.7**
**Comparison of Permanent Party Enlisted Requirements, Manpower Authorizations, and Personnel**

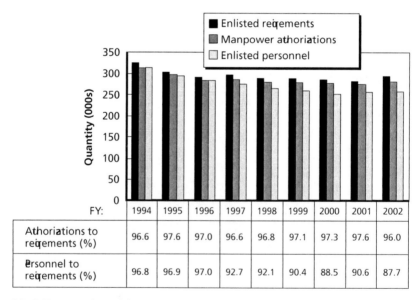

| FY: | 1994 | 1995 | 1996 | 1997 | 1998 | 1999 | 2000 | 2001 | 2002 |
|---|---|---|---|---|---|---|---|---|---|
| Athorizations to reqements (%) | 96.6 | 97.6 | 97.0 | 96.6 | 96.8 | 97.1 | 97.3 | 97.6 | 96.0 |
| Ersonnel to reqements (%) | 96.8 | 96.9 | 97.0 | 92.7 | 92.1 | 90.4 | 88.5 | 90.6 | 87.7 |

SOURCE: Data adapted from Air Force Manpower and Ersonnel Data Systems.
RAND MG492-3.7

overall enlisted personnel-to-requirements ratio averaged 92 percent and was as low as 88 percent in 2000 and 2002. If total requirements had been substituted for manpower authorizations and if SORTS reporting applied to the aggregate Air Force, these years might have warranted P-2 ratings, indicating less-than-full readiness but sufficient people to undertake most assigned missions.

Unfortunately, the absence of process output metrics precludes describing the shortage's effect in terms of workload backlog and tasks not performed.[8] Without definitive output measures, it is difficult to quantify the "hurt" or to determine how well decisions are made, with respect to workload adjustments and productivity, when work centers are short of people. These measures would provide valuable feedback to the human capital system and could help level workforce stress. As an example, in an effort to determine the length of the average military workweek, AFMA collected supervisor-reported data from fall 2002 through winter 2004. The data indicated that some specialties averaged over 15 hours of overtime each week, while some others averaged only 2 to 3 hours.[9] These survey results helped identify 1,000 positions that could be realigned from "less stressed" specialties to "overly stressed" specialties.

## Overall Assigned-to-Authorized Ratio Masks Problems in the Middle Grades

The overall permanent party personnel-to-authorizations percentage declined from 100 in FY 1994 to 91.3 in FY 2002. Figure 3.8

---

[8]  Output metrics are normally recorded during the development of manpower determinants and standards. However, data reflecting military hours worked, units produced, backlog, and tasks not performed are not routinely documented and reported for most Air Force activities (equipment maintenance activities are obvious exceptions).

[9]  AFMA used Web-based techniques and stratified sampling to collect work center supervisors' weekly estimates for the hours worked by assigned personnel. The survey covered 140 specialties across 75 bases. Survey data were collected at 10 to 12 bases for each specialty. The typical base reported data for about 20 specialties. The baseline workweek was about 43 hours.

divides the enlisted grades into three tiers: top three (E-9, E-8, and E-7), middle three (E-6, E-5, and E-4), and bottom three (E-3, E-2, and E-1).[10] The top three and bottom three grades have consistently matched or exceeded the overall percentage, but that is not true for the middle three grades. Since 1997, fill rates for the middle three grades have been less than those of the other tiers. The phenomenon appears to be associated with both disproportional increases in requirements for the middle three grades and earlier enlisted accession policies.

## Distribution of Grades

UMDs document both required and authorized military grades (DAF, 2003d). Required grades are documented to show preferred grades, if grades were unconstrained, given the mission and workload.

**Figure 3.8**
**Enlisted Personnel-to-Authorizations (by tiered grades)**

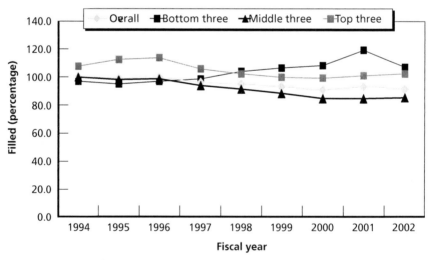

SOURCE: Data adapted from Air Force Manpower and Personnel Data Systems.
RAND MG492-3.8

---

[10] The lowest enlisted grade shown on manpower documents is E-3. E-2 and E-1 may be assigned against E-3 positions.

Authorized grades are constrained to reflect fiscal reality and budgeted grade ceilings. The personnel assignment components use the authorized grades and ignore required grades. Every two to four years, the authorized grades are adjusted in an effort to distribute them equitably among both the commands and career progression groups (CPGs).[11] Commands may not exceed command grade factors, which are derived from the sum of their fixed and fair-share grades, but they may redistribute their allocated grades among CPGs to meet mission requirements. Fundamentally, the military grade-allocation process uses command and CPG factors to convert required grades into authorized grades consistent with the FYDP.

Figure 3.9 shows that, as a proportion of permanent party enlisted manpower authorizations, the middle three grades grew two percentage points between 1994 and 2002. The proportion of the top three grades increased almost 1 percent, while the bottom three decreased

**Figure 3.9**
**Distribution of Permanent Party Enlisted Manpower Authorizations by Grade**

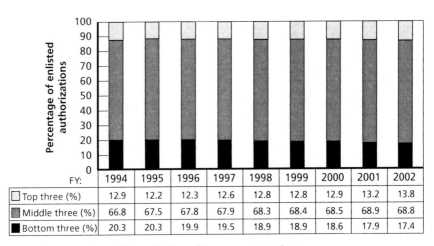

| FY: | 1994 | 1995 | 1996 | 1997 | 1998 | 1999 | 2000 | 2001 | 2002 |
|---|---|---|---|---|---|---|---|---|---|
| ☐ Top three (%) | 12.9 | 12.2 | 12.3 | 12.6 | 12.8 | 12.8 | 12.9 | 13.2 | 13.8 |
| ▨ Middle three (%) | 66.8 | 67.5 | 67.8 | 67.9 | 68.3 | 68.4 | 68.5 | 68.9 | 68.8 |
| ■ Bottom three (%) | 20.3 | 20.3 | 19.9 | 19.5 | 18.9 | 18.9 | 18.6 | 17.9 | 17.4 |

SOURCE: Data adapted from Air Force Manpower Data System.
RAND MG492-3.9

---

[11] CPGs are aggregates of specialties based on the first three digits of the AFSC.

nearly 3 percent. Figure 3.10 shows that the trend among assigned permanent party personnel was the opposite as the authorized grade distribution was creeping upward. The proportion of people actually serving in the middle three grades declined nearly 4 percentage points between 1994 and 2001 before rebounding 1.5 points in 2002. The proportion of people serving in the bottom three grades grew nearly 3.5 points between 1994 and 2001 before dropping 2.5 points in 2002. The top three grade proportion of enlisted personnel increased 0.5 percentage points during this period.

Given each year's end strength, the DoD limits the number of personnel within each service that may serve in the top five enlisted grades. Public law further restricts the number that may serve in the top two enlisted grades. The periodic calibrations of the manpower documents attempt to bring the authorized grades within these limits. The Air Force personnel promotion program targets the same limits when promoting people to fill needs within specific grades (DAF, 1993a). Even with a common target, a gap grew between authorized manpower and assigned personnel in the middle three grades.

**Figure 3.10**
**Distribution of Permanent Party Enlisted Personnel by Grade**

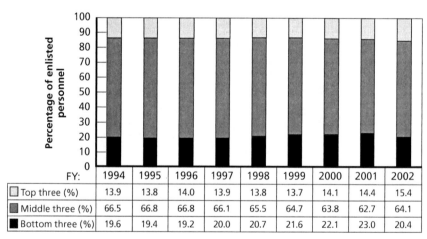

| FY: | 1994 | 1995 | 1996 | 1997 | 1998 | 1999 | 2000 | 2001 | 2002 |
|---|---|---|---|---|---|---|---|---|---|
| ☐ Top three (%) | 13.9 | 13.8 | 14.0 | 13.9 | 13.8 | 13.7 | 14.1 | 14.4 | 15.4 |
| ▨ Middle three (%) | 66.5 | 66.8 | 66.8 | 66.1 | 65.5 | 64.7 | 63.8 | 62.7 | 64.1 |
| ■ Bottom three (%) | 19.6 | 19.4 | 19.2 | 20.0 | 20.7 | 21.6 | 22.1 | 23.0 | 20.4 |

SOURCE: Data adapted from Air Force Manpower Data System.
RAND *MG492-3.10*

## Force Management

One aspect of force management involves predicting the likely effects of recruiting, promotions, and separations on the Air Force's ability to match people to the skills and grades forecast in manpower authorizations. Even in a steady-state environment, with rates and flows nearly identical each year, this is a complex process with complex interactions. In a dynamic environment, such as the force drawdown of the 1990s, the process is even more challenging. During a drawdown, the Air Force faces the major decision of how to balance bringing in enough new people (accessions) to meet future needs against the desire to protect people already in the force.

Figure 3.11 shows that, during the 1990s drawdown, the Air Force weighted the scales more toward reducing accessions. If the Air Force had been in a steady-state environment with accessions equal to losses, the top chart would have shown a gradual stepping down of each column until nearly reaching zero at 30 years. This chart shows that the Air Force had several years, roughly 1990 to 2001, during which accessions were fewer than needed to sustain a force of about 300,000 enlisted personnel, which was the average enlisted end strength from 1994 through 2002. Also, the chart shows a hump starting in year 15, suggesting a preference for retaining people who wanted to build Air Force careers. The net effect is adequate numbers of people in the top and bottom thirds, but a shortage in the middle.

As the lower chart in Figure 3.11 shows, the vast majority of people in the middle grades entered the Air Force during the drawdown period, when accessions were reduced below the level needed to sustain the projected grade and skill profiles. When this is coupled with disproportional increases in manpower authorizations for the middle three grades, a shortage in these E-4 grade and 5-level skills is inevitable, unless other adjustments are made to compensate (i.e., accelerated promotions, improved retention).

## Unit-Level Effects

For a typical Air Force wing, the middle three grades constitute the majority of the enlisted manpower authorizations. People in these

**Figure 3.11**
**Comparison of Annual Accessions to Number of Enlisted Personnel by YOS (tiered by grade)**

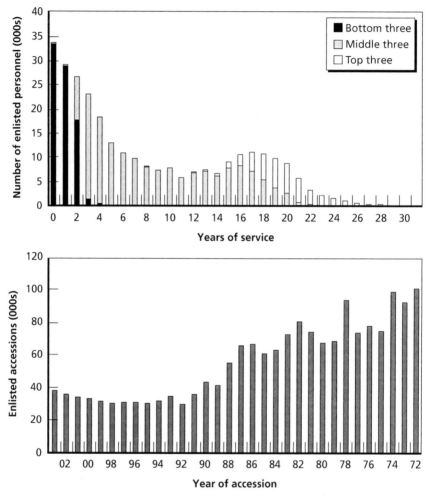

SOURCE: Enlisted personnel data adapted from Air Force Personnel Data System; accessions data adapted from Defense Manpower Data Center.

RAND *MG492-3.11*

grades generate the aircraft, load the weapons, and repair facilities. They also provide OJT to people in the lower three grades. The data in Figure 3.8 show that, since 1997, the Air Force has increasingly had too many people in the lower three grades and too few in the middle three grades. A workforce with this distribution will be less experienced and less productive and will suffer additional workforce stress (see Dahlman et al., 2002).

Figure 3.12 shows that, between 1994 to 2002, the overall average YOS, a proxy for workforce experience, declined from 8.67 to 8.27, with the largest decreases occurring in the middle three grades. The overall average YOS for the middle three grades declined from 9.1 in 1994 to 8.8 in 2002. A closer look shows that the average YOS for E-6s actually increased from 14.6 to 15.9. Conversely, the average YOS for both E-5s and E-4s decreased, from 10.5 to 8.5 for E-5s and from 5.0 to 3.5 for E-4s.[12] Given the decreased accessions, the dramatic decrease in E-5 and E-4 average YOS indicates significant increases in promotion selection rates to E-5 and probably E-6. Even with these increases in promotion rates, the small year-group size as a result of reduced accession levels led to undermanning of the middle-grade authorizations. The undermanning in the middle grades, coupled with the less-experienced workforce (evidenced by the reduced YOS for these personnel), was a severe challenge for the units.

Shortfalls in experienced personnel lead to a less-productive workforce. Junior personnel are tasked to perform jobs normally accomplished by more-experienced senior personnel. Often, less-experienced people will require additional time and may commit more mistakes, resulting in rework. The limited number of senior personnel must

---

[12] The decrease in average YOS for E-4s and E-5s demonstrates the interaction of accession and promotion policies. Generally, promotions up to E-4 are based on time in service, with 36 months being the phase point for sewing on on E-4 insignia. Promotions from E-4 to E-5 and from E-5 to E-6 are competitive and based on promotion selection rates. Given the constant phase point for E-4, the promotion selection rate for E-5 must have increased during this period for average E-5 YOS to decline. (Note: To verify our observation, we checked selective promotion rates and found that E-5 rates were 16.4 percent in 1993 and 63.0 percent in 2002; E-6 rates were 11.3 percent in 1993 and 33.5 percent in 2002.)

**Figure 3.12**
**Average YOS (by grade)**

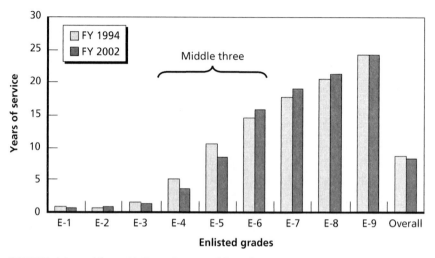

SOURCE: Adapted from Air Force Personnel Data Systems.
RAND *MG492-3.12*

spend more time training and supervising subordinates and less time performing their other duties.

The shortage of journeymen, craftsmen, and OJT trainers appears to have contributed to workforce stress for people filling the middle three positions. Given the gap between the middle third's documented requirements, authorized manpower, and enlisted personnel, they would have needed to work overtime to accomplish the necessary tasks. Several comprehensive measures, such as declining readiness indicators and increased rotational deployments during the study period, would support arguments that at least portions of the Air Force were working harder and longer hours. Unfortunately, no Air Force–wide work-center-level documentation for military hours worked or tasks deferred exists.[13]

---

[13] AFMA's personnel-loading survey, which collects these data, did not start until fall 2002. Biannually, the Air Force conducts an organizational climate survey that asks each respondent to estimate the average number of weekly hours overtime worked, if any.

## Potential Performance Goals, Feedback Sensor, and Force-Shaping Options

Given the trends and patterns identified in this chapter, we offer the potential performance goals and feedback sensors listed in Table 3.1 to help calibrate the performance of the human capital management system.

**Table 3.1**
**Notional Performance Goals, Feedback Sensors, and Force-Shaping Options**

| Performance Goal | Feedback Sensors | Management Options |
|---|---|---|
| A person for every valid enlisted requirement | Assigned-to-requirements ratio | Reengineer processes to reduce requirements |
| | Authorized-to-requirements ratio | Obtain additional military end strength |
| | Requirements-to-end-strength ratio | Obtain funding to shift military requirements to civilian or contractor |
| | | Pare missions to match resources |
| Fully funded pipeline accounts | Actual versus programmed size of pipeline accounts | Ensure that pipeline accounts are properly programmed |
| | | Revise training curricula to reduce pipeline size |
| UMDs match FYDP manpower | Ratios of authorized-to-allocated end strength, by program element code and MAJCOM | Implement manpower changes as directed |
| Faces match spaces | Assigned-to-authorized ratios, by specialty and grade | Reengineer processes to reduce higher-grade requirements |
| | | Adjust promotion policies |
| | | Implement CPG adjustments as directed |

# CHAPTER FOUR

# A Closer Look: Trends in Selected Specialties

To understand how these manpower and personnel issues have affected Air Force MAJCOMs and their units, we took a closer look at 12 specialties. This involved performing a historical analysis of selected wings, functional areas, and specialties to identify specific trends and patterns in generating requirements, funding authorizations, and assigning personnel. We performed this analysis for data covering the FYs 1994 through 2003. However, the Air Force stop-loss program, instituted on May 2, 2003, temporarily halted all separations and retirements of both officers and enlisted personnel in selected specialties. Because of this program and the mobilization of forces for Operation Iraqi Freedom, the number and distribution of enlisted personnel in the Air Force were artificially higher in FY 2003, and so we excluded them from our analysis.

## Analysis Procedure

The analysis included the following steps:

1. Develop selection criteria for both bases and functional specialties.
2. Select functional areas and specific wings for study.
3. Determine appropriate manpower standards for the selected specialties.
4. Collect the requirement, authorization, and assignment data for the selected specialties and wings.

5. Calculate manpower requirements from the standards and compare them to requirements, authorizations, and personnel assignments for each functional area.

### Selection Criteria and Selected Bases and Specialties

We selected 16 Air Force bases (AFBs) for the analysis, choosing at least one but preferably two major bases from each MAJCOM.[1] The chosen bases and their commands are shown in Table 4.1. We endeavored to select bases that covered a wide spectrum of conditions but were thought to be reasonably representative of the range of installations in the command. We identified the host wing for each base and focused our analysis on the manpower and personnel within host wing organizations.

We selected a set of seven functions including 12 specialties for the analysis. These were chosen from a list of functions that commands had indicated were being stressed by manpower shortages.[2] These functional areas and the selected specialties are shown in Table 4.2.

We chose specialties with relatively large numbers of personnel concentrated within one or two functions and not widely spread across several functions. We also selected functions that were present in most or all of the bases and host wings of interest. The functional account codes that correspond with these functional areas and specialties are shown in Table 4.3.

Table 4.4 shows the matrix of bases and specialties that defines the combinations of functional areas and bases investigated in the study.

### Manpower Standards and Data Sources

As stated in AFI 38-201, unit manpower requirements should be based on manpower determinants, including manpower standards, aircrew

---

[1]   Of the MAJCOMs, ACC has the largest number of major bases (15), so we selected one additional ACC base. Other commands, such as AMC and AFSPC, have about ten major bases each.

[2]   When the sample was selected, the sponsors indicated the problems were likely to exist across the force, both in the aggregate and in virtually all specialties.

ratios, and LCOM. Using manpower standards implementation codes in the manpower data system, we found that roughly half of the current requirements are based on manpower standards and their inherent workload factors.

Within the Air Force, AF/A1M and AFMA have responsibility for developing and maintaining manpower standards (DAF, 2003d). Each command may also develop command-specific standards for unique missions or situations. These standards are quantitative expressions of manpower requirements in response to varying levels of workload. The development of standards involves reviewing all options for perform-

Table 4.1
**Bases Selected for Historical Analysis**

| Installation | Command |
|---|---|
| Aviano AFB | U.S. Air Forces in Europe (USAFE) |
| Barksdale AFB | Air Combat Command (ACC) |
| Eielson AFB | Pacific Air Forces (PACAF) |
| F.E. Warren AFB | Air Force Space Command (AFSPC) |
| Hurlburt AFB | Air Force Special Operations Command (AFSOC) |
| Keesler AFB | Air Education and Training Command (AETC) |
| Langley AFB | ACC |
| McGuire AFB | Air Mobility Command (AMC) |
| Misawa AFB | PACAF |
| Peterson AFB | AFSPC |
| Pope AFB | AMC |
| Randolph AFB | AETC |
| Robins AFB | Air Force Materiel Command (AFMC) |
| Shaw AFB | ACC |
| Spangdahlem AFB | USAFE |
| Tinker AFB | AFMC |

**Table 4.2**
**Functional Areas and Specialties in the Analysis**

| Function | AFSC | Specialty |
|---|---|---|
| Aviation Maintenance | 2A3 | Tactical avionics systems maintenance |
| Aviation Maintenance | 2A5 | Aerospace maintenance |
| Aviation Maintenance | 2A6 | Propulsion and aerospace ground equipment |
| Aviation Maintenance | 2A7 | Materials, structure, and survival |
| Aviation Maintenance | 2W0 | Munitions systems |
| Aviation Maintenance | 2W1 | Aircraft armament systems |
| Aviation Fuels | 2F0 | Fuels |
| Fire Protection | 3E7 | Fire protection |
| Explosive ordnance disposal (EOD) | 3E8 | Explosive ordnance disposal |
| Readiness | 3E9 | Readiness |
| Security Forces | 3P0 | Security forces |
| Military Personnel | 3S0 | Personnel |

ing a mission, including the use of government civilians or contracted manpower. If military personnel must perform the function, the process may consider which component (active, guard, or reserve) is most appropriate. The standard quantifies the manpower resources required and the anticipated workload for each product or service supplied by the function. It may also identify variances to this basic requirement—location-specific additions or subtractions associated with different types of missions, technology, or environmental issues.

Most of the current standards were last revised in the early to mid-1990s, so they must be used with caution by the commands. Current practice, confirmed through interviews with personnel involved in determining command manpower requirements, seems to be to use incremental workloads as the basis for modifying current requirements rather than starting from the generally out-of-date standards. As indicated in Chapter Three, Air Force units are not restricted to these stan-

**Table 4.3**
**Functional Account Codes**

| Function | Code | Title |
|---|---|---|
| Aviation Fuels | 41d1 | Fuels Management Flight |
| EOD | 44ed | Explosive Ordnance Disposal |
| Fire Protection | 44ef | Fire Protection |
| Maintenance | 22b1 | Sortie Generation Flight |
| Maintenance | 23b1 | Fabrication Flight |
| Maintenance | 23c1 | Propulsion Flight |
| Maintenance | 23d1 | Accessories Flight |
| Maintenance | 23f1 | Aerospace Ground Equipment Flight |
| Maintenance | 23g1 | Armament Systems Flight |
| Maintenance | 23h1 | Munitions Flight |
| Military Personnel | 16b1 | Military Personnel Flight |
| Readiness | 44eb | Air Base Operability |
| Security Forces | 43a1 | Standards and Evaluation |
| Security Forces | 43b1 | Administration and Reports Flight |
| Security Forces | 43c1 | Operations Flight |
| Security Forces | 43d1 | Training and Resources Flight |

dards for determining manpower requirements. Aircraft maintenance functions, for example, predominantly use LCOM as the basis for their requirements. The LCOM results are then modified to account for local factors and command priorities. In this analysis, we used the manpower standards for all functional areas except aircraft maintenance. The standards and their dates of last revision are shown in Table 4.5.

Each standard may specify a core unit composition and one or more workload factors that are used in man-hour equations to calculate manpower requirements, although a standard will occasionally define a constant manpower requirement, with variances, for all bases. The

**Table 4.4**
**Functional Areas Present at Selected Bases**

| AFB | Aircraft Maintenance | Aviation Fuels | Security Forces | Military Personnel | EOD | Fire Protection | Readiness |
|---|---|---|---|---|---|---|---|
| Aviano | X | X | X | X | X | X | X |
| Barksdale | X | X | X | X | X | X | X |
| Eielson | X | X | X | X | X | X | X |
| F.E. Warren | | | X | X | | X | X |
| Hurlburt | | X | X | X | X | X | X |
| Keesler | | X | X | X | | X | X |
| Langley | X | X | X | X | X | X | X |
| McGuire | X | X | X | X | X | X | X |
| Misawa | X | X | X | X | X | X | X |
| Peterson | | | X | X | | X | X |
| Pope | X | X | X | X | X | X | X |
| Randolph | | | X | X | | X | X |
| Robins | | | X | X | | X | X |
| Shaw | X | X | X | X | X | X | X |
| Spangdahlem | X | X | X | X | X | X | X |
| Tinker | | | X | X | | X | X |

**Table 4.5**
**Manpower Standards Used in the Analysis**

| Functional Area | Manpower Standard | Last Revision |
|---|---|---|
| Aircraft fuel | Fuels Management (41D1) | May 3, 1996 |
| EOD | EOD Flight (44ED) | March 7, 1997 |
| Fire protection | Fire Protection Flight (44EF) | September 11, 1996 |
| Military personnel | Military Personnel Flight (16B1) | May 16, 1997 |
| Readiness | Readiness Flight (44EB) | March 9, 2000 |
| Security | Security Police Squadron (43XX) | December 12, 1994 |

specific workload factors and equation coefficients may vary between commands within a given standard. Each of the six standards used in our analysis uses one or more of the following workload factors:

1. existence of a weapons platform at the installation
2. primary aircraft inventory equivalent
3. total gallons of aviation fuel issued
4. installation manpower authorizations[3]
5. base population[4]
6. military base population
7. authorized military population served.

Using data obtained from Air Force data systems, we determined the values of all workload factors for each functional area by FY at each installation. In particular, we used file parts A, B, and D of UMDs drawn from the Air Force Manpower Data System (MDS) for requirements and funded authorizations. We obtained personnel assignment information for the years of interest from the Air Force's E300Z report,

---

[3]  Depending on the standard, authorizations may include all installation and tenant military, freshman class cadets, permanent change of station students, and base support service contract employees.

[4]  Base population may include contract man-year equivalents, Air Force tenant units, non–Air Force military tenant units, additional contractor personnel, and monthly pipeline student authorizations, where applicable.

which is an extract from the Air Force Advanced Personnel Data System. We extracted aircraft and weapon system data in extracts from the Air Force Program Database. These data extracts include both aircraft authorizations by unit and base and programmed flying hours.

We obtained the desired data for each year of interest and processed the information as required so it could be used in this analysis. Processing steps included converting the data to a more-useful format; correcting obvious typographical errors; and making the unit identification, organizational location, and other variables consistent from one year to the next.

### Calculate and Compare Requirements, Authorizations, and Assigned Strengths

We determined the total requirements, funded authorizations, and assigned personnel for each specialty using the combinations of specialty code and functional account code for each year at each installation. We then calculated the manpower requirements for each specialty using the appropriate manpower standards, workload factor values, and variances for each installation of interest. In this analysis, we examined both authorized and assigned personnel at the installations to see how much the actual workload factors differed from programmed workloads and whether these differences affected the manpower requirements in any functional area.

With this information for each functional area and specialty, we could compare calculated manpower requirements with the stated requirements and funded authorizations found in the MDS and with the assigned personnel data. We were looking for trends within and across specialties and across commands over time, particularly to determine the extent of personnel shortages and whether these shortages have become worse in recent years.

## General Trends

The appendix provides summaries of how each specialty fared over the period of interest. In this section, we compare trends across specialties and commands.

### Funding Rate for Specialties

Figure 4.1 compares the specialties in terms of the percentage of stated requirements that has been funded by the commands (the funding rate). From the figure, it is clear that the commands have, on average, funded over 95 percent of wing requirements throughout the period. EOD has had the lowest percentage of funding, and maintenance has had the highest. With the exception of the apparently anomalous value in 1994, the funding rate has been remarkably consistent, until the dramatic drop for the security and readiness specialties in 2002. Possible explanations for this drop are the lag between the development of new requirements and their funding and the addition of special requirements as a result of the AEF supplemental requirements process and, later, the terrorist attacks.[5]

### Funding Rate for Commands

In addition to looking at funding rates for specialties, we should also consider how the funding rate has varied across the commands. Figure 4.2 shows the overall funding rate by command for all specialties included in the analysis. Again, in general, the funding rate remains at 95 percent or higher for most commands, with PACAF being some-what higher and AFMC lower than the average. The decrease in the funding rate for PACAF and AMC in 2002 indicates that PACAF and AMC were the primary commands whose increased security require-ments were not funded in that year. Still, the overall pattern shown in

---

[5]   As the Air Force migrated to the AEF concept, about 5,000 manpower authorizations were realigned from various activities (Panama closure, field operating agency reductions, etc.) to functions supporting AEF deployments. Operations in support of the global war on terror led to the realignment of authorizations from specialties under less deployment stress to those experiencing more.

**Figure 4.1**
**Funding Rate by Specialty**

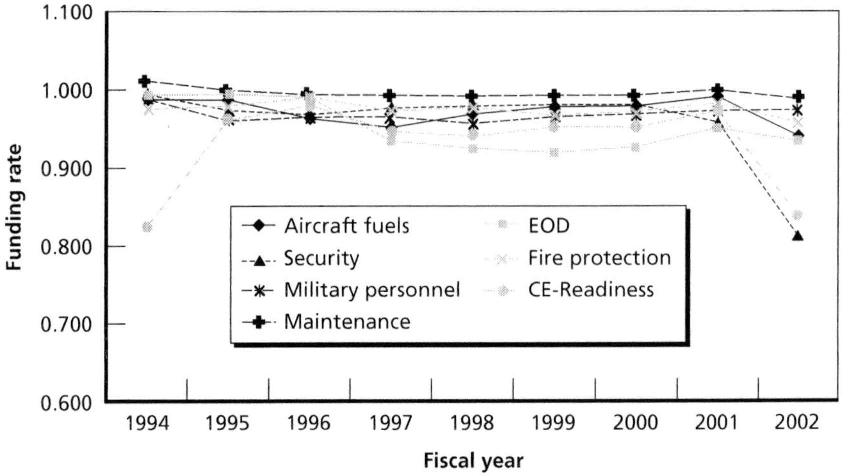

the figure indicates that, with few exceptions and although the commands have different funding rates, the rates are quite consistent across time for each command.

In addition to the two declines in 2002, there appears to be a slight general reduction in the funding rate in 2002 for most commands and most specialties. The Air Force has instructed the commands in recent years to report their requirements more fully (DAF, 2003d, para. 2.8),[6] which may be the cause for these apparent decreases.

### Fill Rate for Specialties and Commands

Although the funding rate is important to the commands and the wings, they are in many ways more concerned about shortages in personnel to fill authorized positions. The fill rate is the ratio of assigned personnel to funded authorizations and, as such, measures how well the Air Force

---

[6]   During our interviews, several MAJCOM manpower directors indicated that this policy received additional emphasis starting in the late 1990s.

**Figure 4.2**
**Funding Rate by Command**

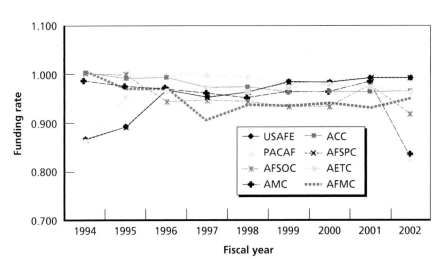

can match approved manpower authorizations with actual personnel. It does not help the wings to have high funding rates if there are no personnel to assign to the funded positions. Figure 4.3 shows the historic trend of fill rates for all commands by specialty. Figure 4.4 gives the fill rates by command, summed over the specialties of interest.

As Figure 4.3 shows, the fill rate for most specialties has declined slowly but steadily over the period. Only for security forces has it remained constant or increased through FY 2002. Although there is more variation in the curves, the same conclusion can be drawn from the fill rates by command shown in Figure 4.4. The average decrease in fill rates for these specialties and commands between FY 1994 and FY 2002 is somewhere between 7 and 10 percent.

## Assignments as a Proportion of Requirements

If we look instead at assignments as a proportion of requirements, the results are consistent. Figure 4.5 shows the ratio of assigned personnel to requirements by specialty. This information shows a strong and

**Figure 4.3**
**Fill Rate by Specialty**

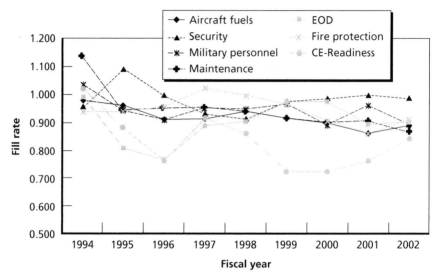

**Figure 4.4**
**Fill Rate by Command**

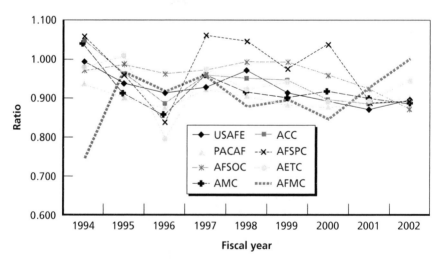

**Figure 4.5**
**Assignments as a Proportion of Requirements by Specialty**

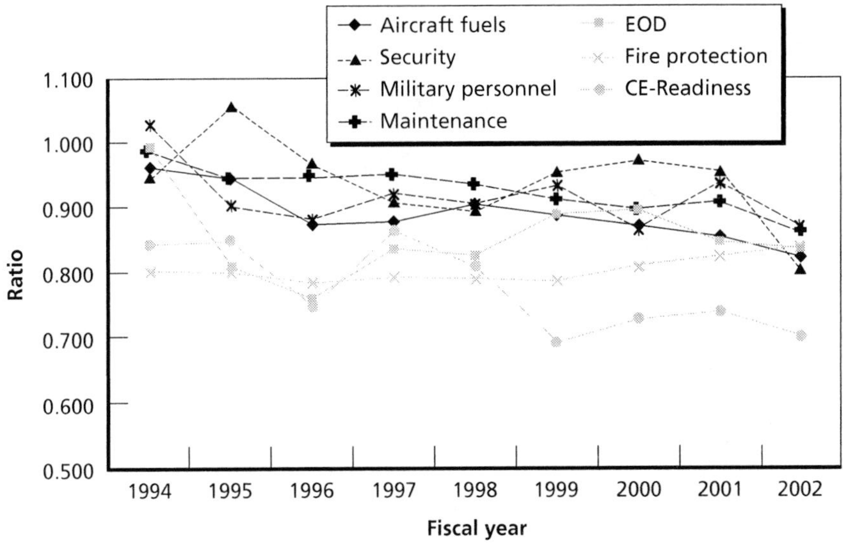

steady decrease in the ratio over time for most specialties. On average, the ratio decreased by more than 13 percent over the period, with
greater declines in recent years. However, the curves have high variability, and some functions declined far less. These are, most notably, fire
protection overall and security forces, military personnel, and aviation
maintenance before the FY 2002 increases in requirements.

**Manpower Standards and Workload Factors**
In theory, the wings should use Air Force or command manpower
standards, LCOM, or aircrew ratios to determine their manpower
requirements across functional areas (DAF, 2003d). In practice, the
data indicate that the use of standards varies by function or specialty.
This is shown in Figure 4.6, which plots the ratio of MDS requirements to the requirements determined using the manpower standards
for each of the relevant functions. As the figure makes clear, some

**Figure 4.6**
**Requirements as a Proportion of Manpower Standards**

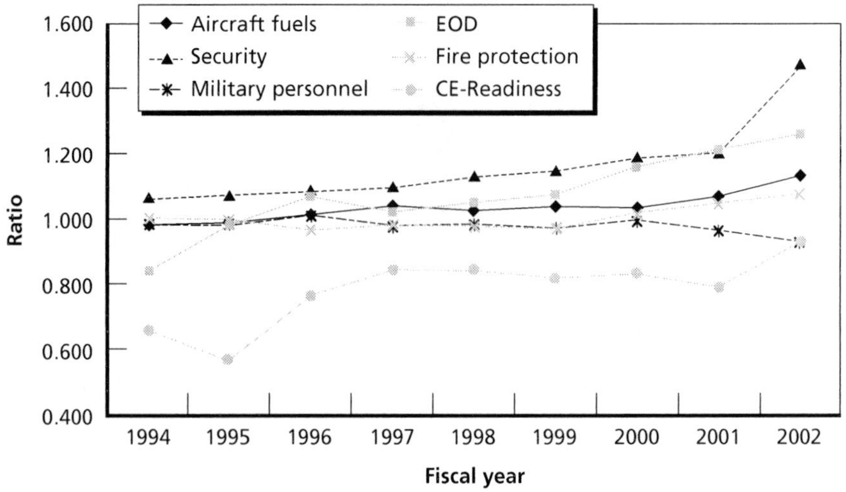

MDS requirements, particularly those for security and EOD, deviated by more than 20 percent from the manpower standard. In every case, the requirements differ from the standards by more than 5 percent, and the differences seem to be increasing. Because of the procedures and coordination required to change the requirements stated on the manpower documents, we accepted the deviations from the standard as *prima facie* evidence that the requirements are genuine and that the standard is ceasing to adequately reflect total needs. This suggests that the manpower standards need to be updated, if only to give wing manpower offices more guidance in the process. The Air Force had started updating the manpower standards using process reengineering. That effort has been terminated in favor of capability benchmarking techniques. The Air Force manpower leadership believes these will produce more-useful manpower determinants more expeditiously.

As more evidence that the manpower standards need to be updated or revised, we can examine the correlation between changes in programmed workload factors and actual manpower actions.[7] Figure 4.7 shows this correlation for the aviation fuels specialty at Barksdale AFB. The figure plots the percentage changes in workload factor (weighted programmed aircraft inventory), manpower standard, required manpower, funded authorizations, and assigned personnel.

It is clear from this information that there is little or no correlation between changes in the workload factor and requirements, authorizations, or assigned strength. Although the weighted programmed aircraft inventory decreased by 28 percent in FY 1996, and the manpower standard dictated a 7-percent reduction, the manpower requirement initially decreased by only 6 percent. Moreover, it subsequently increased to 6 percent over the original base-year level. Authorizations decreased slowly after the initial decline, then gradually returned to the

**Figure 4.7**
**Workload Factors and Manpower Actions, Aviation Fuels Specialty, Barksdale AFB**

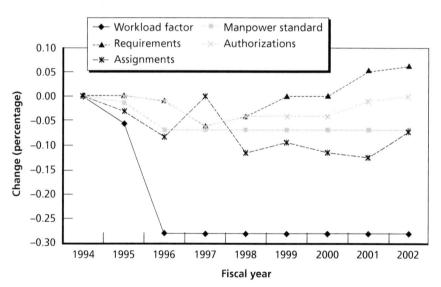

---

[7]  We analyzed differences between actual and programmed workload factors and, for the most part, found that the differences were inconsequential. For observations reported in this document, we used only programmed workload factors.

FY 1994 level. Finally, the assigned personnel varied more irregularly but, by FY 2002, had returned to the level calculated by the manpower standard, which may be more of a coincidence than a direct result of applying the standard.

The same information is plotted for Langley AFB in Figure 4.8. In this case, the pattern is more consistent. The required manpower changes generally followed changes in the workload factor. Moreover, the funded authorizations and assigned personnel also generally followed the same pattern with a delay in implementation.

Unfortunately, Langley is the exception, not the rule, in this analysis. Most of the other wings more closely resemble the Barksdale pattern, with its lack of correlation.

## Workload Insufficiently Considered

So far we have focused on the fundamental issues of manpower standards and requirements determination, funding rate, and fill rate. As deficiencies grow in these areas, the more likely it becomes that workforce stress will exist. However, these are not the only potential sources of workforce stress that Air Force organizations face. At least two others may not have been given sufficient attention. First, although in many units the number of assigned personnel may be close to their funded authorizations, the distribution of the personnel by skill level or grade may differ significantly from what is authorized. An excess of inexperienced personnel will create additional training demands for senior personnel and reduce the capability and productivity of the organization. Second, manpower requirements have traditionally been determined assuming some nominal demand for temporary duty (TDY) assignments, such as training. In recent years, operating under the AEF concept, Air Force deployment requirements have been high, placing a much larger TDY burden on support units. In this subsection, we will discuss each of these two issues.

**Figure 4.8**
**Workload Factors and Manpower Actions, Aviation Fuels Specialty,**
**Langley AFB**

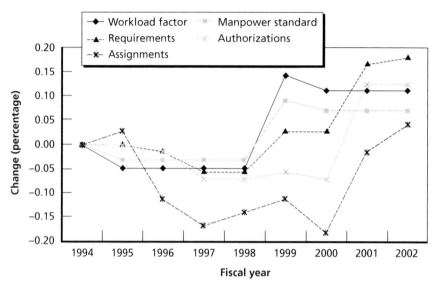

## Training Load

In this section we discuss two specialties: security forces and fire protection. We performed comparable analyses for the other ten specialties and found somewhat similar patterns.

Airmen undergoing initial formal school training are assigned a skill level of 1. When they complete this training and arrive at their first duty station, their skill level increases to 3, and they continue training on the job. These are the personnel in the lower three grades described in Chapter Three. The more-senior and -skilled personnel in the specialty (those with skill levels of 5 or 7) generally occupy the middle three grades and supervise the OJT for the junior personnel while performing their normal duties. If there are too many personnel in the lower three grades for the number of available trainers, this OJT load can become a burden and can interfere with normal activities. For purposes of our analysis, we have defined the training load for a specialty at a wing as the relative numbers of personnel or positions with skill levels of 1 or 3 (trainees) to personnel or positions with skill levels of 5 or 7 (trainers).

The anticipated training load for a specialty in an organization can be expressed as the ratio of trainees to trainers for funded authorizations. The actual training load is the value of the ratio for assigned personnel. Figure 4.9 compares these two ratios for the security forces specialty over the period of interest. It is clear that the actual training load, shown by the assigned curve, remains close to the planned load until 1997, after which it increases to become about 50 percent greater than the planned training load in FY 2002.

This means that the skilled personnel must spend more of their time training the less-skilled personnel and also suggests that trainees are most likely performing tasks that normally require a 5-level specialist. As a consequence, middle-grade noncommissioned officers (NCOs) are spending more time training subordinates, less time doing, and probably more time correcting errors of the less-experienced personnel.

**Figure 4.9**
**Training Load for Security Forces**

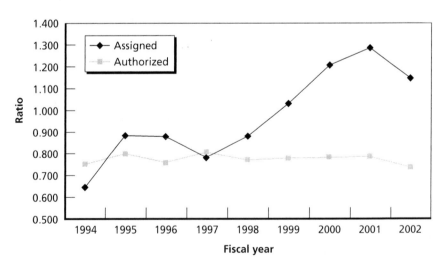

This would reduce efficiency and productivity and increase the risk of error in the performance of duties. This would further add to the stress and level of frustration on the part of both the junior and middle-grade personnel. Middle-grade NCOs must either jump in and do today's work themselves while ignoring the training of junior personnel or must train the junior people to do the work in the future while assisting them in doing today's work.

Although the training load for security force personnel has increased over time, this increase has not been uniform across the different wings and commands. Figure 4.10 shows the planned and actual training loads for security forces in the wings of interest in FY 2002. Although there are large variations among wings and commands, all the selected wings have higher-than-planned training loads.

Figures 4.11 and 4.12 show the corresponding training load information across time and wings for the fire protection specialty. In this

**Figure 4.10**
**Training Load for Security Forces by Installation**

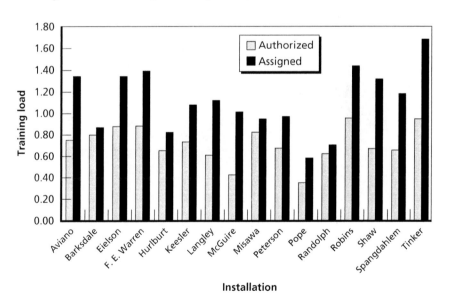

Installation

**Figure 4.11**
**Training Load for Fire Protection**

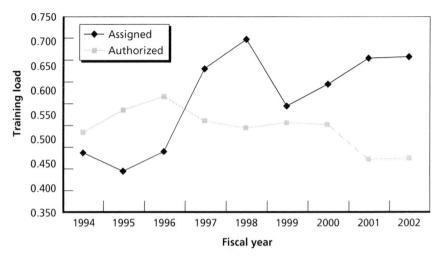

**Figure 4.12**
**Training Load for Fire Protection by Installation**

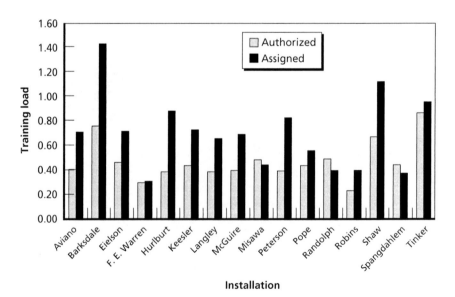

case, the actual training load is less than the planned training load through FY 1996, then quickly grows until it stabilizes in FY 2001 and FY 2002 at 45 percent above the planned level. Figure 4.12 shows that the training load varies dramatically across installations and is actually less than the planned loads at Misawa and Spangdahlem but far more than the planned loads at Barksdale, Hurlburt Field, Peterson, and Shaw.

## Temporary Duty and Deployments

Under the EAF concept, the Air Force today deploys large numbers of personnel, including those in expeditionary combat support. During deployments, workloads for most functions at a base may not decrease significantly, although the personnel remaining at the base to perform this work may have been reduced. Most manpower standards were developed or last revised in the mid-1990s, when deployments were smaller and less frequent. Consequently, the standards do not take into consideration that many functions may be seriously understaffed during deployments.

To investigate the extent to which this phenomenon may be occurring, we examined the TDY data for the specialties and wings selected for our historical analysis. We compared the TDY days for May 2002 through April 2003 with the corresponding TDY days for April 1997 through March 1998. For both periods, we calculated the Air Force–wide average number of TDY days for each specialty. We looked only at TDY periods greater than 60 days and calculated the percentage of personnel in each period who were on TDY for that duration.

The results of this analysis are shown in Table 4.6. In the table, the lightly shaded cells represent functions and wings for which the percentage of personnel on long TDY increased between 1998 and 2003. The darkly shaded cells represent situations in which the percentage of personnel not only increased but also exceeded the Air Force–wide percentage for that specialty. It is clear from these data that increases in long TDY percentages were prevalent in these specialties during the past four years. The increases were almost across the board at Barksdale, Hurlburt Field, Langley, McGuire, Pope, and Spangdahlem, bases that belong to ACC, AFSOC, AMC, or USAFE. As a consequence of these

**Table 4.6**
**Percentage of Personnel with More Than 60 TDY Days (May 2002–April 2003)**

| AFB | 2A3 | 2A5 | 2A6 | 2A7 | 2W0 | 2W1 | 2F0 | 3P0 | 3S0 | 3E7 | 3E8 | 3E9 |
|---|---|---|---|---|---|---|---|---|---|---|---|---|
| Aviano | 5.7 | 7.9 | 6.1 | 8.8 | 14.4 | 4.2 | 11.0 | 8.2 | 11.1 | 10.1 | 68.4 | 30.0 |
| Barksdale | 23.1 | 17.4 | 18.8 | 26.6 | 21.3 | 25.9 | 37.4 | 9.2 | 21.2 | 47.9 | 20.0 | 16.7 |
| Eielson | 34.4 | | 22.8 | 24.3 | 5.6 | 37.1 | 37.9 | 24.3 | 8.3 | 37.9 | 50.0 | 22.2 |
| F.E. Warren | | | | | | | | 1.3 | 10.3 | 35.1 | | |
| Hurlburt | 33.3 | 29.9 | 26.3 | 30.6 | 39.3 | 28.2 | 29.2 | 23.9 | 15.1 | 22.4 | 4.5 | 40.0 |
| Keesler | | 0.0 | | | | | 3.8 | 16.2 | 10.0 | 0.0 | | 50.0 |
| Langley | 32.4 | 2.8 | 29.1 | 33.6 | 40.0 | 42.3 | 42.7 | 22.9 | 9.9 | 35.2 | 43.5 | 20.8 |
| McGuire | 16.7 | 45.8 | 39.0 | 31.8 | 35.7 | | 46.8 | 37.7 | 9.2 | 37.8 | 33.3 | 30.8 |
| Misawa | 12.0 | | 5.7 | 4.3 | 10.5 | 13.1 | 7.4 | 4.5 | 14.0 | 10.6 | 0.0 | 41.7 |
| Peterson | | | | | | | | 14.7 | 6.6 | 15.2 | | 25.0 |
| Pope | 32.7 | 42.0 | 36.4 | 28.3 | 47.4 | 38.6 | 23.0 | 22.8 | 18.0 | 22.0 | 58.3 | 0.0 |
| Randolph | 2.9 | 16.7 | 4.5 | | | | | 27.9 | 6.0 | 18.2 | | 22.2 |
| Robins | 3.7 | | 11.1 | 13.3 | 12.5 | 0.0 | 3.4 | 13.6 | 9.2 | 11.8 | | |
| Shaw | 11.3 | 14.3 | 12.8 | 15.9 | 17.0 | 11.3 | 20.0 | 16.6 | 13.4 | 23.6 | 10.0 | 10.0 |
| Spangdalem | 33.6 | 0.0 | 26.8 | 25.8 | 32.0 | 33.3 | 63.1 | 5.4 | 8.4 | 45.2 | 26.1 | 18.2 |
| Tinker | 33.3 | 24.0 | 22.8 | 25.3 | | | | 12.2 | 10.4 | | | |
| Air Force–wide | 18.8 | 23.4 | 17.5 | 16.3 | 20.4 | 20.9 | 26.4 | 15.4 | 9.9 | 23.7 | 25.4 | 22.2 |

increased TDY loads, the workload in expeditionary combat support functions at these installations has to be absorbed by the remaining nondeploying personnel, which increases workforce stress.

The Air Force is moving toward developing a dynamic, flexible, and expeditionary force structure. Accordingly, future manpower requirements will be based on capability and developed through a capability-based manpower standards (CMS) process.[8] This process is being designed to capture total force manpower requirements while focusing on the Air Force's expeditionary requirements. Our results suggest that such an approach is clearly needed. This will be difficult and will be constrained by other factors, such as manpower ceilings and budget limits, but it may be possible to level the stress on the non-deploying personnel in all the functions.

## Observations

In this chapter, we examined a number of important issues by looking at a historical picture of Air Force requirements, funded authorizations, and assignments for a selection of bases and specialties. We also examined the issues related to skill-level mix within specialties and extended periods of TDY, including deployments.

In our examination of selected specialties and installations, we found that actual manpower requirements and changes in requirements have weak or no correlation with the manpower standards or changes in programmed workload factors. This suggests the manpower standards and/or the programmed workload factors are not capturing other sources of workload variability. One example of workload not adequately reflected in existing manpower standards is AEF deployments. Another example is the magnitude of the training workload for middle-grade personnel. These discrepancies reinforce the current perception that the existing manpower standards are generally out of date and can differ significantly from the requirements stated by the wings.

---

[8]   CMS is discussed in more detail in Chapter Five.

The data also indicate that the wings have been reasonably consistent in funding their requirements at about 95 percent. However, the Air Force has not been as successful in maintaining fill ratios for these authorizations. These ratios have generally declined over the past ten years, reflecting the trends revealed in Chapter Three—an increasing tendency for manpower authorizations to exceed available end strength, creating unachievable expectations.

The number and length of TDY periods (including deployments) seem to have increased in recent years. The manpower standards do not take periodic deployments (as seen under the AEF concept) into consideration when determining requirements. We do not know whether the commands have been including deployment loads in their requirement determinations, but it is unlikely, given that most requirements (with some exceptions) have not increased significantly in the past few years.

Finally, the middle three grades in some specialties are currently undermanned, and the lower three grades are overmanned in most wings. For several reasons, this increases the demands on middle-grade personnel and seems to be causing more acute work-related stress in these specialties.

## Additional Performance Goals, Feedback Sensors, and Force-Shaping Options

Recall that in Chapter Three we offered four notional performance goals with possible feedback sensors and force-shaping options. In this chapter, we add four additional goals (see Table 4.7).

**Table 4.7**
**Notional Performance Goals, Feedback Sensors, and Force-Shaping Options**

| Performance Goal | Feedback Sensors | Force-Shaping Options |
|---|---|---|
| Minimize excess unit-level training burden | Assigned versus authorized junior (skill levels 1 and 3) to middle (skill levels 5 and 7) ratios | Reduce inflow of junior personnel |
| | | Increase inflow of people with 5 and 7 skill levels |
| | | Increase amount of schoolhouse training |
| | | Add more field training detachment capability at the bases |
| Account for both expeditionary and in-garrison workload | Proportion of manpower requirements based on CMS | Reevaluate military-civilian-contractor mix |
| | Percentage of specialty deployed more than 120 days in 20 months | Calibrate schoolhouse training to help make trainees ready for deployment sooner |
| Minimize gaps between programmed workload and actual workload | Differences between programmed workload and actual workload | Reevaluate workload planning factors |
| | | Provide workforce augmentation |
| Minimize the amount of excess overtime worked | Amount of documented overtime worked | Adjust resources to be commensurate with actual workload |
| | | Adjust planned capability to be commensurate with resources actually available |

# CHAPTER FIVE

# A More-Comprehensive Human Capital System

The trends in Chapters Three and Four suggest that "standard, Air Force–wide" human resource policies and practices are, in reality, neither standard nor Air Force–wide. The functional communities, working with the individual components of the human capital system, and the MAJCOMs attempt to chart the best paths for their collections of specialties. However, as discussed in Chapter Two, few, if any, managers gain a comprehensive view of the interactions between the various human capital components and their cumulative effects on wing-level manpower authorizations and the workforce available to accomplish the mission. Additionally, fragmented procedures and compartmented computer systems make it nearly impossible to routinely monitor the overall health of the Air Force's human resources and their contributions to achieving missions and goals.

In recent years, the Air Force has launched several initiatives that could afford a more-comprehensive, systems-oriented perspective and ameliorate some of the issues raised in Chapters Two, Three, and Four. In this chapter, we first summarize ongoing Air Force initiatives, then offer recommendations for moving even further toward realizing the benefits of a holistic system.

## Recent Changes in Air Force Human Capital Management

In recent years, the Air Force has launched several initiatives to move toward a more-holistic human capital system. In this section, we discuss six that should help achieve and maintain an appropriate balance between manpower authorizations, skill levels, and PERSTEMPO.

### Air Force Personnel Strategic Plan (FY 2004–2009)

The latest Personnel Strategic Plan, published in 2003, reflects systems-oriented thinking. As with most strategic plans, it provides a vision; outlines goals, objectives, and performance measures; assigns responsibilities; and establishes provisions for institutionalization. The plan provides a framework linking personnel, training, and manpower strategies with "broader institutional guidance, and the Air Force's mission, vision, core values, core competencies, and distinctive capabilities" (DAF, 2003a, p. i).

This linkage recognizes that the human capital system is a critical part of a larger system and provides approaches for pursuing better horizontal alignment at all organizational levels: strategic, operational, and tactical. The plan adopts an expansive description of the personnel life cycle: define, renew, develop, sustain, synchronize, and deliver. This comprehensive perspective recognizes that the personnel life cycle includes defining requirements for human capability and synchronizing the planning, programming, investment, and development of human capital. This more-inclusive view should provide opportunities to improve the vertical alignment of human capital system components. The plan contains multiple goals and objectives with metrics to measure performance. The goals exhibit equifinality,[1] characteristic of open systems, suggesting they may be accomplished with diverse inputs and various internal activities. The metrics, when fully developed, will allow the goal champions to evaluate the difference between their current positions and desired futures through gap analysis—a form of feedback. The plan establishes a structure for developing, updating, implementing, and overseeing accomplishment of the goals and objectives, facilitating the inevitable adjustments as the internal and external environments change.

---

[1]  In general systems theory, the concept of *equifinality* emphasizes the potential for the same goal or end point to be reached through multiple paths or means.

Several of the issues identified in Chapters Two, Three, and Four stem from a fragmented view of human capital management. As one example, the manpower system appears to have adjusted authorizations without the benefit of feedback concerning the ability of the training and assignment systems to meet those requirements.[2] If authorizations are added and if there are no people to fill them, the operational units are merely given unachievable expectations. The personnel strategic plan depicts human capital management as a dynamic system with interconnecting subsystems in which the actions of one subsystem have implications for the actions of the others and in which these implications are given appropriate consideration. This framework encourages the exploration of interactions between human capital components.

The metrics and other elements needed to realize the full effects of the Personnel Strategic Plan are still being developed. It remains to be seen whether most or all strategically important human resource management outcomes can be accurately and comprehensively measured and whether the results will powerfully and routinely drive policy and action. The plan has promise, but much more remains to be done.

## Total Force Development

Operationally, the concept of total force development is still maturing; however, it has tremendous unifying and vertical alignment potential. Jumper (2003, p. 1) states that "Force Development is all about getting the right people in the right job at the right time with the right skills to fight and win in support of our national security objectives, now and in the future." The goal is to better prepare the total force—active duty, Air Reserve component, and civilian workforce—to successfully lead and accomplish rapidly evolving global missions while fulfilling personal and professional expectations to the greatest extent possible consistent with mission accomplishment (DAF, 2004a). The concept emphasizes both the relational and synergistic natures of the first four

---

[2] The manpower specialists were only required to coordinate with the personnel specialist if the proposed change would occur within approximately nine months. During our interviews we found no evidence of macro-level analysis to determine if aggregate manpower demands were supportable or sustainable.

elements of the personnel life cycle: define, renew, develop, sustain. The first steps in integrating people into Air Force operations are defining the required capabilities, then organizing the skill sets required to produce those capabilities. Force renewal ensures that the Air Force will continue, over time, to acquire a workforce with the capabilities to execute its mission. Development takes individual capabilities and, through education, training, and experience, produces skilled, knowledgeable, and competent airmen. Sustainment balances retention and investments in force development with cost-effectiveness and evolves in response to changing operational requirements. Coordinated strategic planning guides the force-development elements to produce competencies rooted in operational capabilities required for current and future missions.

The total force-development concept could help attenuate several trends presented in Chapter Four (e.g., consistent disconnects between manpower requirements and authorizations, an expanding gap between the number and type of manpower authorizations and the people assigned, and a growing unit-level training burden). A major contribution was establishing the Force Development Council to provide an institutional perspective on Air Force–wide force-development issues. The council's members review the health of the force and provide corporate-level policy guidance and investment strategy recommendation. Another contribution is the establishment of development teams to provide oversight of personnel development to meet both functional family and corporate Air Force requirements. However, to be effective, these teams need reliable, integrated information about the current and future demand and supply of human capital. To meet this need, a force-development support office was established at AFPC. A subtle, yet significant, contribution is the use of institutionally agreed-upon terminology among the human capital components and across functional communities.[3] This should reduce disconnects caused by resources accounted for differently depending upon what type of specialist is doing the counting.

---

[3] One example is the agreement between the manpower and personnel components on how to code and count students assigned against permanent party authorizations.

## Capability-Based Manpower Standards

Appropriately defining requirements is the foundation of human capital management; the Air Force has launched development of CMSs as the cornerstone of the manpower requirement determination process. The CMS process is a workload approach for defining manpower requirements in terms of category (military, civilian, reserves, contractor), numbers, specialties, skill levels, and grades. The workload approach focuses on the amount and type of workload or capability the organization anticipates. Simply stated, the CMS process seeks to link manpower requirements to an approved Air Force task force concept of operations (CONOPS) via capabilities defined in the Master Capabilities List.[4] Given an appropriate context and a desired output, determined through an appropriate set of scenarios, manpower and other resource requirements are linked to subcapabilities, which are linked to capabilities, which are linked to CONOPS. In contrast to existing Air Force manpower standards, which rarely include deployment requirements, the CMS process starts with the desired deployment capability and sequentially adds others (e.g., in-place combat, directed missions). Institutional and sustainment manpower requirements, which may be additive to capability-derived requirements, are determined using alternative methods. The CMS process uses Web-based data collection and measurement techniques to permit rapid and timely evaluation of information from all applicable locations. Thus, the manpower requirements for each installation will be based on its mission and unique characteristics. This approach again contrasts with the development of conventional Air Force manpower standards, which

---

[4] The Air Force has six approved task force CONOPS that support capabilities-based planning—a central theme for defense planning. Each CONOPS identifies capabilities an Air Force Task Force will need to accomplish its mission for joint force commanders. During the Cold War era, the Air Force focused primarily on countering the capabilities and threat posed by a known enemy. The transition to task force CONOPS focuses on desired effects against specific threats, with the goal of providing robust, flexible forces capable of meeting a wide variety of threats, rather than an "optimal" force for a narrow set of threats. See Davis (2002) for extensive discussion of capabilities-based planning. The Master Capabilities List, still evolving, provides a "menu" from which people tasked to develop task force CONOPS can choose required capabilities. Each capability is defined and further divided into varying levels of subcapabilities.

were typically based on a small number of locations using averaging, regression, and correlation techniques to approximate requirements for unmeasured locations. Once the CMS process is fully operational, AFMA indicates that CMSs will be developed and/or updated in less than six months, compared to the more than two years required for developing conventional manpower standards.

If the CMS process performs as advertised, the commands and bases will have updated, reliable manpower standards to help estimate their manpower needs.[5] The standards for functions addressed in this study, indeed in most of the published manpower standards, were developed during the early to mid-1990s and need replacing. As noted in Chapter Four, actual workload demands and expeditionary deployments appear to have been given insufficient consideration in currently published standards. The latter deficiencies were largely driven by inadequate consideration of contingency and wartime requirements during the development of mid-1990s manpower determinants. The CMS process corrects these deficiencies by starting with the sizing of manpower requirements for capabilities needed to perform missions for combatant commanders. Additionally, currently published standards were constructed using averages from relatively few locations. Units often complained that the averages were not applicable for their locations. Under the CMS process, every location will have manpower standards constructed for its mission and tailored to its specific circumstances. The technology used to develop CMSs facilitates rapid, yet comprehensive, development of manpower determinants and should preclude relying on badly outdated standards. As the manpower requirements cornerstone, the CMS process should yield more-accurate and -timely manpower determinants that are directly tied to Air Force capabilities.

---

[5]   AFMA, working with the functional communities, is preparing a schedule to develop CMSs for all applicable specialties. Priority is being given to the more "stressed" specialties.

## Manpower Programming and Execution System

The Air Force is fielding the Manpower Programming and Execution System (MPES) to modernize its manpower data system.[6] In Figure 2.1, we depicted how the HQ USAF manpower function flows data to and from the F&FP system. Similarly, we depicted how the command and base-level manpower functions flow data to and from HQ USAF. MPES replaces both the HQ USAF MDS (HAF MDS) and the command MDS.[7] The Web-based system provides a single relational database for the FYDP (programming, planning, budgeting) and unit authorization file (i.e., UMD data). This will facilitate real-time comparison between the FYDP and the unit authorization file ("checkbook balancing") and continuous billet management down to the base level (e.g., base-level personnel can instantly see changes programmed at HQ USAF, and HQ USAF programmers can instantly see changes made to UMDs). The system will have internal checks and balances to eliminate intermediate transactional and verification inputs.

As presently used by the U.S. Army and the Central Intelligence Agency, MPES has interfaces with budgeting and personnel management systems that could help streamline the transfer of data between various manpower, personnel, and budgeting activities.

## Total Human Resource Managers' Information System

Designed specifically for use by career-field managers, the Total Human Resource Managers' Information System (THRMIS) is a Web-based decision-support software application that mines data from various

---

[6]  MPES is a variant of a government-owned system that has been fielded by both the Army and the Central Intelligence Agency. MPES achieved initial operational capability on March 31, 2005, with full operational capability planned for March 31, 2006.

[7]  HAF MDS is an HQ USAF–level resource accounting and management information system that contains all F&FP manpower data. HAF MDS is used to process and transmit manpower allocation data to the commands. Similarly, it accepts and consolidates manpower requirements and authorization data from the commands and combines the data into the Consolidated Manpower Database. MDS is a separate accounting and information system that exchanges data with HAF MDS and contains manpower requirements and authorization data to support command headquarters and base-level activities. The Resource Manpower Management system replaces these systems.

human capital repositories.[8] It collects and warehouses manpower and personnel data for the total force: active duty (officer and enlisted), Air Force Reserve, Air National Guard, and civilians. THRMIS digests quarterly manpower (demand) and monthly personnel (supply) files to create statistical abstracts and tables to fuel interactive Web displays. Career-field managers and action officers use these interactive displays and queries to help analyze and assess the health of specific career fields; functional communities; and, collectively, the entire Air Force.

Prior to the development of THRMIS and such other utilities as the Interactive Demographic Analysis System and the Retrieval Application Web site provided by AFPC, most HQ USAF and command functional and career-field managers were unable to accurately determine the total number of human resources (active duty, reserve, guard, and civilian) that were associated with activities they were tasked to oversee. By collecting data from dissimilar data systems and organizing them in simple, comparative, and meaningful ways, THRMIS and these utilities help improve managers' diagnoses of the human resource health of activities they oversee. Better health assessments at these levels will help senior leadership make more-informed decisions about the distribution and allocation of overall Air Force human resources.

### Merger of Manpower, Personnel, and Education and Training Career Fields

The merger of these career fields should help remove barriers between three critical human capital functions: manpower planning, personnel management, and training management. The merger appears to be more than symbolic. Indeed, it appears intentionally designed to alleviate barriers that have hampered cross-functional problem solving. Senior leaders and implementers are rooting out processes that are incongruent with systems-oriented thinking by changing the cul-

---

[8]   THRMIS emerged from an initiative, started in November 1999, to support the Total Force Career Field Review, which the Chief of Staff of the Air Force mandated. During this review, for the first time ever, all designated functional managers were required to analyze the health, structure, and sustainability for their portion of the Air Force workforce across all categories of human resources (active duty, Air Force Reserve, Air National Guard, civilian, and contractor) and personally brief the chief.

ture with such initiatives as overhauling schoolhouse course content, realigning resources, reengineering processes, and substituting technology for transaction labor. This involves changing not just processes but also attitudes and perceptions, the quality of products, the ways decisions are made, and a multitude of other factors.

In concert with the merger, those charged with overseeing human resource activities are reassessing its role, architecture, and infrastructure. At every level, greater emphasis is being placed on making human resource professionals strategic partners. This strategic partnership affects the full array of services, such as the design of work positions, hiring, pay and rewards, performance, development, and appraisal systems. The objective appears to be to integrate decisions about people with decisions about the results an organization is trying to obtain—by integrating human resource management into the planning process and emphasizing human resource activities that support mission goals.

## Additional Changes Are Needed

The ongoing changes in Air Force human resource management are indicative of a major paradigm shift, from a stress on expertise in transactions and retail-level actions to a stress on wholesale-level actions, such as the development and optimal use of human capital. The latter perspective requires human resource professionals who have the abilities and tools to advise senior leaders and managers on how best to use all available human capital assets to accomplish current and future missions. These professionals, given their organizational level, should be able to fine-tune human capital policies and programs to better align human resources with the organization's objectives. They will need the ability to collect and analyze information quickly from multiple sources to define current and future mission and workforce needs, identify gaps, and develop actionable recommendations to close the gaps. To help fulfill this emerging role, we recommend six changes in addition to those listed in the previous section.

## A More-Comprehensive Description of Requirements

To have a clear picture of human resource requirements, data must be collected in three dimensions: workload, workforce, and competency. The Air Force's manpower community has concentrated on the workload dimension. The personnel community has stressed workforce attributes. In recent years, the Air Force has begun to address the subject of workforce competencies, especially at the senior leader level, through its force-development structure, and the Air Force human resource management community seems to be feeling its way toward a beddown of responsibilities for managing competency issues.

The workload dimension addresses the amount and type of work the organization anticipates and uses this information to project the number of resources (people, skills, and grades) that will be needed to perform the work. The objective is to identify critical work the workforce must perform to accomplish the mission. The relevant data include cycle time, task time, volume, performance parameters, and cost measures.

The workforce dimension examines the current workforce and occupations and projects the numbers, characteristics, and policies into the future to assess how well future needs will be met. Current workforce profiles are the starting point. The next step is to project the current workforce into the future using appropriate policies and rates for accession, promotion, and attrition. The results yield insights into existing or emerging gaps, workforce sustainability, and succession issues.

The competency dimension focuses on sets of characteristics (encompassing skills, knowledge, abilities, and personal attributes) that, taken together, are critical to accomplishing the work and achieving the organization's objectives. Normally, the competency studies assume the organization has already given adequate consideration to workload and workforce requirements and can focus not only on the number of people but also on the competencies that will be needed for individual and organizational success.

Each dimension is crucial for determining future human capital needs, identifying gaps, and implementing solutions so that the Air Force can continue to accomplish its mission, goals, and objectives.

Historically, decisionmakers have concentrated on one dimension in isolation from the others. Often, while conditions in one dimension may improve, problems are created or aggravated in the other dimensions.

In our view, a more-comprehensive description of requirements is needed. Historically, the Air Force has generally thought of manpower requirements from a workload perspective. However, to fully understand Air Force manpower requirements, it is imperative to integrate workload, workforce, and competency dimensions within manpower requirement processes.

Models and tools that integrate these dimensions would help crystallize issues, identify embedded assumptions, and surface potential unintended consequences. Similarly, these models and tools could help human resource professionals and career-field managers develop better gap-closure recommendations by addressing such questions as these: Are there equally effective and/or efficient workforce solutions that do not create sustainability issues? Given planned force-structure changes, what changes are needed in competency development to ensure the appropriate types and quantities are available to meet future needs?

### Greater Use of Dynamic Simulation Models

Systems-oriented organizational constructs require an institutional understanding of what happens when multiple systems intersect. Without this knowledge, each system will attempt to optimize its own performance independent of the other systems and even pull in contradictory directions.[9] Symptoms of this suboptimization include an endless spiral of superficial quick fixes, recurring problems despite quick fixes, worsening difficulties in the long run, and an ever-deepening sense of powerlessness to change outcomes. Suboptimization often occurs in complex systems, such as the Air Force's human capital system, when the interactions are too complicated to reliably replicate by intuition. *Simulation modeling* is a useful approach for developing an understanding of the interaction of parts of a system and of the

---

[9]   See key guiding ideas for learning organizations, especially the section on the primacy of the whole, in Senge et al. (1994, pp. 24–27).

system as a whole. A simulation model is an abstract representation of an existing or proposed system designed to identify and understand the factors that control the system and/or to predict the future behavior of the system. Almost any system that can be quantitatively described using equations and/or rules can be simulated.

The Air Force has a plethora of very useful static, compartmented human resource models and tools. They create snapshots and projections showing what happens if all other activities, especially those in other human resource components, are held constant. These models and tools represent the state of the human capital system at a particular time or when time simply plays no role. These models and tools are useful for setting goals and evaluating static characteristics, such as accession goals, promotion targets, and personnel strength statistics. However, most of these models and tools offer limited, if any, understanding of how the problems will change if the planning assumptions are incorrect or if the other systems are incapable of making the necessary adjustments. Static, compartmented analysis tools rarely afford penetrating insights into how the interactions between systems or the passage of time caused the present problems or contributed to the solutions. For this, the Air Force will need to develop dynamic simulation models. In dynamic simulation, the models represent systems that are evolving over time. The objective is to understand how the system might evolve, predict the future behavior of the system, and determine what can be done to influence future behavior.

Dynamic simulation shifts the thinking to the processes of change rather than mere snapshots. Real-world problems in complex organizations seldom have a single right answer. Instead, there are normally several feasible actions. Each action will likely produce some of the desired results over a specified period and will probably have some unintended consequences. Dynamic simulation provides a way to recognize and demonstrate the ramifications of alternative policies and plans without having to experiment with the real systems. These models and tools are used to evaluate policies and scenarios that are time-dependent and involve complex interactions between components. These analyses extend static models and show changes, trends, and patterns over time. They would allow the user to uncover knowledge across the human resource spectrum through computer experimentation and to receive immediate feedback. Succinctly stated, these models and tools could be used to draw conclusions about the risks and benefits associated with alternative policies and plans.

Dynamic simulation models could also be used to train and educate human capital managers. In complex systems, without the aid of simulation models, many who believe they are using systems thinking may often merely be jumping to conclusions. As Herbert Simon (1957, p. 198) stated,

> The capacity of the human mind for formulating and solving complex problems is very small compared with the size of the problem whose solution is required for objectively rational behavior in the real world, or even for a reasonable approximation to such objective rationality.

Dynamic simulation models often reveal that the most appropriate actions are counterintuitive and sometimes are the subtlest. Scenarios could be constructed to help managers understand the underlying rules for various human capital practices. Managers could learn when taking no action, letting the system make its own corrections, yields the best results. Other scenarios could teach when and where to intervene in the human capital system to be most effective and under what conditions. Collectively, these scenarios could help demonstrate what ideas will work and produce good results with fewer side effects.

## Measuring and Providing Systemwide Feedback

In Chapter Two, we emphasized that a simple concept, the *feedback loop*, is critical when adopting a comprehensive, systems-oriented approach toward human capital management. Feedback loops show how actions can reinforce or balance each other. Effective feedback loops enable the institution to learn what patterns recur again and again, what cycles and cycle times are common, what consequences are associated with selected actions, and how to mitigate differences between planned and actual outcomes. Appropriately constructed feedback loops help the institution see the deeper patterns underlining the events. This increased insight helps decisionmakers find the points in the cycle where adjustments or changes could be most effective.

The human capital feedback loop should aid in diagnosing the fit between the Air Force's overarching strategies and current or planned human capital strategies and practices. It should provide performance feedback on both the outputs of internal human capital processes and outcomes of the external overarching strategies to continuously improve strategic performance and results. While not jettisoning traditional performance goals—eight additional goals were proposed in Chapters Three and Four—more attention should be given to developing strategic metrics demonstrating links between human capital management and Air Force performance. One example might be a measure of how effective the human capital components are in maximizing the number of available expeditionary deployment days. Are military requirements in nondeploying specialties being appropriately reduced? Is training being conducted in a manner that makes more deployment days available? Are medical availability codes being managed in a manner that ensures eligible personnel are available for deployments?

### Resuscitating the Requirement Determination Process

The requirement determination process, one of the foundational blocks of the human capital system, has been atrophying and needs to be revitalized. The data in Chapters Three and Four raised serious questions about the adequacy of published manpower determinants. The determinants used in our sample did not reflect the expeditionary nature of today's Air Force. Neither did they reflect the training burden that was being imposed on middle-rank NCOs. Commands made changes in manpower authorizations that were not consistent with these determinants, suggesting that the determinants were losing their utility. The growing disparity between manpower authorizations and assigned personnel argues for better integration of the workload and workforce dimensions of requirements determination.

The Air Force should fully implement its CMS process as quickly as possible. This process will link manpower to approved Air Force task force CONOPS. This process starts with the desired deployment capability and sequentially adds others (e.g., in-place combat, directed missions). While determining the quantity of manpower needed, recommendations are formulated regarding the most appropriate category of manpower resources (military, civilian, reserves, contractors). Web-based data collection and measurement techniques facilitate developing determinants for each location, rather than relying averages based on relatively small samples. If the process works as promised, these determinants will be developed and/or updated in less than six months instead of the more than two years previously required. In conjunction with implementing the CMS process, a workload-based methodology, we recommend integration of workforce sensitivity analysis techniques to determine the sustainability of proposed workforce configurations.

### Establishing a Single Set of Manpower Books

Legacy computer systems resulted in the Air Force having at least three sets of manpower books, which contributed to discrepancies between the advertised and actual numbers of people available for wing-level missions. One system, HAF MDS, provides HQ USAF–level resource accounting and management information and contains all F&FP manpower data. A separate manpower system, MDS, periodically exchanges data with the HAF MDS system and is used by the commands to document their requirements and support other activities. On a monthly basis, the MDS system provides data to the Military Personnel Data System (MilPDS)—a third system—which the assignment and training communities use to provide people to units distributed throughout the world. These three systems, with their different users and slightly different accounting rules, make it difficult to keep the manpower books in balance. For example, HAF MDS reflected the OSD-levied reductions but the commands did not fully implement them in MDS. As another example, some parts of the pipeline accounts are visible only at the HQ USAF level. As still another example, parts of the pipeline accounts are accounted for differently in the MDS and MilPDS systems, resulting in different estimates for the number of people available for wing-level missions.

The Air Force is fielding MPES to replace both HAF MDS and MDS, which will address two of the three computer systems. We recommend the Air Force explore ways of better integrating MPES data into the personnel assignment and training systems. The U.S. Army and the Central Intelligence Agency have created totally integrated systems. While MPES, or variants thereof, will address the computer issues and provide one set of books, a culture has developed that permits and, unintentionally, rewards commands and units that overspend their accounts. Processes and mechanisms should be developed that encourage a continuous reconciliation of the manpower books to minimize overspending.

### Addressing Skill-Level Imbalances

At the wing level, the more-senior and -skilled military personnel occupy the middle three grades and supervise OJT for the junior personnel in addition to performing their normal duties. If there are too many personnel in the lower three grades for the number of trainers, this OJT load can become a burden and can interfere with other mission activities. To illuminate these issues, the Air Force collected personnel loading data during FYs 2003 and 2004. These data reveal a statistically significant correlation between locations with specialties having higher numbers of semiskilled personnel and increased overtime hours reported in the specialties.

We recommend that the Air Force establish a metric that tracks the planned versus actual training burden imposed on wing-level personnel. The metric could be as simple as the one used in Chapter Four, which compared the ratio of authorized semiskilled personnel to skilled personnel with the actual ratio of semiskilled personnel to skilled personnel. As these ratios reach various trigger points, commanders would be able to request such actions as TDY assistance, contractor or reserve component support, workload relief (i.e., permission to produce fewer sorties), field training assistance, or more schoolhouse training for trainees.

### Summary

Our research argues that the Air Force will benefit significantly from a more-comprehensive, well-integrated system of systems for managing its military human capital. The Air Force is already starting to achieve many of the benefits of such an approach: leveraged interactions, increased efficiency, and better strategic alignment. While applauding the ongoing efforts, we offer additional changes to buttress the transformation. Many may view the additional changes as daunting. The purpose of presenting them is not for people to embrace them posthaste but to encourage efforts to find ways to pursue them meaningfully.

# CHAPTER SIX

# Conclusions and Recommendations

This study examined the cumulative effect of the Air Force human resource system on wing-level manpower, skill levels, and PERS-TEMPO. The overarching conclusion is that a more-holistic approach to human capital management is needed to maintain the appropriate balance between manpower, personnel, skill levels, and PERSTEMPO. As acknowledged in Chapter Five, the Air Force has embarked on several initiatives moving toward a more-holistic system. Our research identifies additional actions needed to facilitate progress toward such a system, alignment between human capital components, and improved internal efficiency. This chapter summarizes the conclusions and recommendations presented in this report.

## Conclusions

Our research and analyses led to five major conclusions:

- A comprehensive, systems-oriented human capital perspective is essential. Many of the issues identified during this study appear rooted in a lack of strategic direction compounded by fragmented approaches to human resource management.
- The Air Force's process for determining manpower requirements needs resuscitation. The data in Chapters Three and Four raise serious questions about the adequacy of published manpower determinants, especially given the expeditionary nature of today's Air Force.

- The Air Force needs one set of manpower books. Legacy computer systems resulted in the Air Force having at least three sets of manpower requirements. This contributed to discrepancies between the manpower authorized for wing-level missions and the actual number of people available.
- Skill-level imbalances affect productivity and contribute to workforce stress. If there are too many personnel in the lower three grades relative to the number of middle-grade trainers, the OJT load can become a burden and can interfere with other mission activities.
- Poor internal feedback between components of the human capital system impedes high system performance. During our interviews at both the HQ USAF and MAJCOM levels, we found little evidence of feedback mechanisms between components of the human capital system.

## Recommendations

Several recommendations emerge from our research and analyses:

- Implement an integrated manpower requirements architecture that considers workload, workforce sustainment, and workforce competencies.
- Make greater use of dynamic simulation models to better understand the intersections of the manpower, personnel, and training subsystems.
- Develop internal feedback loops between components of the human capital system that could be used to identify gaps in capabilities and/or misalignments between the manpower, personnel, and training activities.
- Implement the CMS process as quickly as possible.
- Field MPES as a means of eliminating multiple sets of books, and explore ways to improve integration of MPES data into the personnel assignment and training systems.

- Establish and track metrics that compare planned against actual training burdens imposed on wing-level personnel.

The next research step is to help the Air Force operationalize the recommendations and the various performance goals, feedback sensors, and management and force shaping options. If these recommendations are implemented in concert with ongoing initiatives, the Air Force should have a better-integrated human capital system yielding leveraged interactions, synchronized roles, and better strategic alignment.

# Manpower and Personnel Trends by Specialty

For each specialty included in our review, we determined how four ratios changed during the period examined:

1. the number of required personnel from the MDS to the number calculated from the manpower standard
2. the number of funded authorizations to the number from MDS requirements
3. the number of assigned personnel to the funded authorizations
4. the number of assigned personnel to the number from MDS requirements.

## Aviation Fuels

The mission of the aviation fuel flight is to manage, store, and distribute petroleum products, oils, lubricants, missile propellants, and cryogenic products (DAF, 1996). These units consist primarily of personnel with the fuel management AFSC, 2F0. Although other units at an installation may have one or two fuel management personnel, almost 99 percent of the personnel in this specialty work in the aviation fuels management flight.

Figure A.1 shows the historical pattern of manpower and personnel ratios for the aviation fuels specialty. From Figure A.1, it is clear that the requirements stated in the MDS have been increasing faster than

**Figure A.1**
**Manpower and Personnel Ratios for Aviation Fuels**

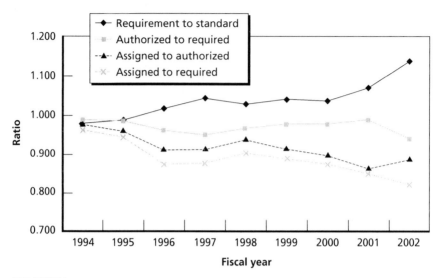

RAND *MG492-A.1*

those that would be calculated from the manpower standard. This is not surprising because the relevant standard was last revised in 1996 and may no longer be appropriate for calculating manpower requirements. Two other trends are also apparent from this figure. First, although the commands have continued to fund about the same percentage of requirements (ratio of authorized personnel to stated requirements), the fill rate (assigned to authorized) has decreased steadily. Second, the ratio of assigned personnel to requirements has decreased even faster, dropping to 82 percent for FY 2002. This ratio is a measure of both the relative priority that the commands place on this specialty and the extent to which the Air Force can provide the personnel required by the commands.

## Aviation Maintenance

In the aviation maintenance functional area, we examined six specialties, as shown in Table 4.2. These specialties can be found in a number of different functions in a typical wing, but 85 percent of them are located in the functional accounts that were included in the analysis. Figure A.2 shows the historical pattern of manpower and personnel ratios for the selected aviation maintenance specialties. Note that there is no graph for the ratio of MDS requirements to the manpower standard requirements. For these maintenance specialties, all requirements are calculated using the LCOM approach, rather than manpower standards.

The commands have been funding virtually all their manpower requirements for aviation maintenance personnel. It is also apparent that a smaller and decreasing percentage of these funded authorizations have actually been staffed with personnel, as the ratio dropped from about 100 percent in FY 1994 to 86 percent in FY 2002. An examination of the numbers indicates that this is more a problem of increasing requirements that were not filled, rather than a decrease in assigned personnel.

**Figure A.2**
**Manpower and Personnel Ratios for Aircraft Maintenance**

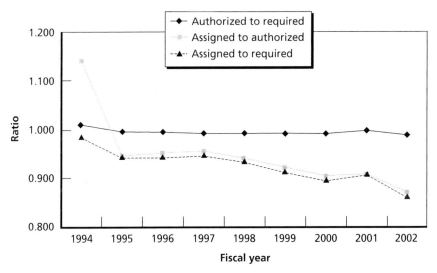

## Explosive Ordnance Disposal

The mission of the EOD flight is to protect people, resources, and the environment from the effects of hazardous explosive, chemical, biological, incendiary, and nuclear ordnance, including criminal and terrorist devices (DAF, 1997b). Flight personnel also locate, identify, and disarm or neutralize explosive hazards. All enlisted personnel with the EOD specialty (3E8) are found in this flight.

Figure A.3 shows the trend in manpower and personnel ratios for EOD. It would appear from this figure that the manpower standard for EOD required revision in FY 1997. During the late 1990s, the Air Force implemented rigorous procedures for adding manpower requirements to UMDs; therefore, we assume that requirements that exceed manpower standards were appropriately justified. After the revision process, the standard worked reasonably well for no more than one or two years before again diverging from the requirements stated in the UMD.

**Figure A.3**
**Manpower and Personnel Ratios for EOD**

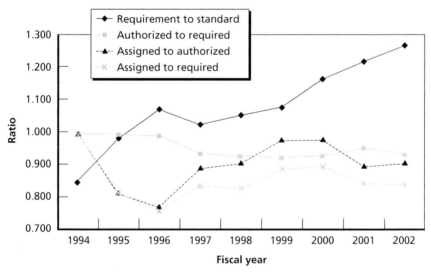

The figure again shows that the Air Force has been funding a fairly constant percentage of the stated requirements. On the other hand, the percentage of authorizations that has been manned has varied significantly over the period. After decreasing to about 80 percent in FYs 1995 and 1996, the percentage increased to almost 98 in 1999 and 2000, but has since declined to only 90 in 2002. Compared to stated requirements, the number of assigned personnel has fallen recently, to just over 82 percent.

## Fire Protection

The fire protection flight protects life, resources, and the environment not only from fires but also from nonordnance hazardous material and disasters during both war and peace. Virtually all personnel in this flight are firefighters, and more than 99 percent of firefighting specialty (3E7) authorizations are found in the fire protection flight.

Figure A.4 shows the historical trend of the manpower and personnel ratios for the firefighting specialty. As with other specialties, the figure indicates that the manpower standard for firefighters has become increasingly less accurate for determining requirements in recent years. The figure also shows that the Air Force has continued to fund between 95 and 99 percent of the commands' stated requirements. In spite of this, the percentage of authorized positions actually filled with personnel has decreased almost steadily since FY 1997. In FY 2002, assigned personnel increased to a little above 90 percent, but only 87 percent of the required personnel were actually present.

## Military Personnel

Personnel specialists (3S0) can be found in a number of different functions scattered throughout the wing. The majority, however—more than 55 percent—are located in the military personnel flight, which consists almost exclusively of personnel in this specialty.

**Figure A.4**
**Manpower and Personnel Ratios for Fire Protection**

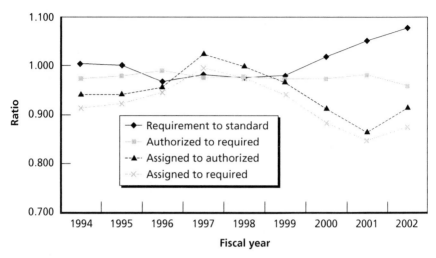

RAND *MG492-A.4*

Figure A.5 shows the historical manpower and personnel ratios for military personnel specialists. In this specialty, the figure indicates that the manpower standard has remained relatively close to the manpower requirements determined by the commands. It also indicates that the Air Force has continued to fund more than 95 percent of these requirements. Finally, although the ratio has varied by a few percent over the period of interest, the figure shows that assignments have generally remained between 90 and 95 percent of funded authorizations since FY 1994, dropping to 89 percent in FY 2002.

## Readiness

The readiness flight provides contingency support services by managing installation disaster preparedness, engineer emergency force, and air operability programs. The flight prepares the wing to mitigate the effects of incidents caused by nature, accident, war, or operations other than war (DAF, 2000). All enlisted personnel in readiness flights are in this enlisted specialty (3E9), and 96 percent of all personnel in this specialty are in readiness flights.

Figure A.6 shows the trends in the manpower and personnel ratios for the readiness specialty. The curves in this figure vary far more than the curves for other specialties, primarily because the number of personnel in this specialty is much smaller. The average readiness flight consists of ten or fewer personnel, so small changes in absolute numbers appear to be large percentage changes.

In this specialty, the figure indicates that actual requirements are generally smaller than those predicted using the manpower standard. As with other specialties, the Air Force has funded at least 95 percent of the stated MDS requirements, except in FY 1994 and FY 2002. It is not clear why the percentage dropped in FY 2002, but it may be associated with a September 11th–related increase in requirements of about 15 percent. The figure also indicates that the ratio of assigned personnel to authorized manpower positions has varied significantly over the

**Figure A.5**
**Manpower and Personnel Ratios for Military Personnel**

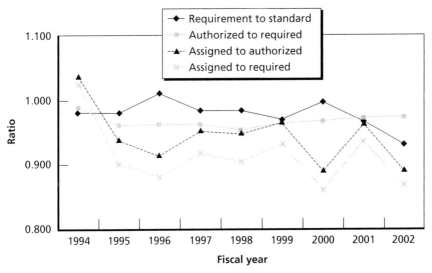

**Figure A.6**
**Manpower and Personnel Ratios for Readiness**

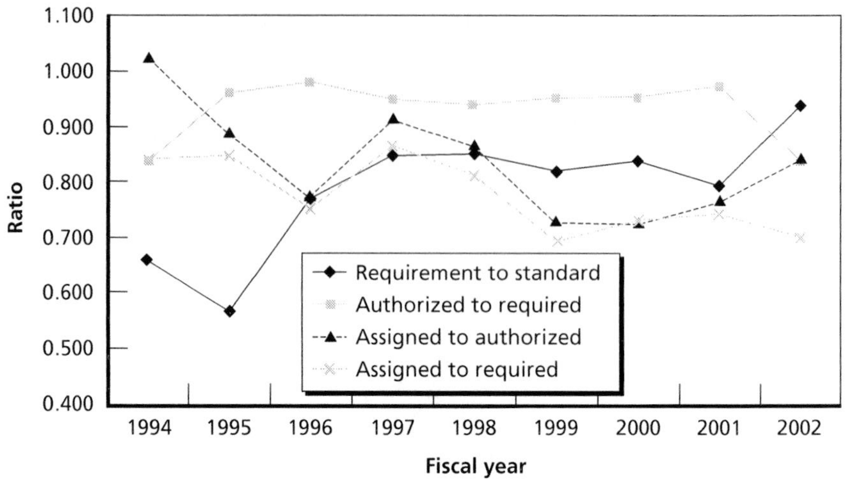

period, from a low of 72 percent to a midperiod high of 91 percent. With this variation, it is also clear that the number of available personnel has not generally been adequate to fill the available positions.

## Security

Although enlisted personnel in the security forces specialty (3P0) are found in several different functional areas, almost 95 percent of them are located in security forces units. These units have multiple functions, including maintaining law and order; developing and maintaining detection programs; providing ground weapon training; and managing installation security, information security, and crime prevention programs (DAF, 1994).

Figure A.7 shows how the manpower and personnel ratios for enlisted security personnel have varied over the period of interest. In this specialty, it is clear that stated requirements have been increasing gradually but remained within 20 percent of those calculated using the manpower standard until FY 2002. The significant increase in MDS requirements in that year may have been associated with increased security concerns after the September 11th terrorist attacks or may have been part of an EAF supplemental requirement determination. As the decrease in the funded authorization ratio indicates, these requirements did not become funded authorizations. It is also clear from the figure that the percentage of requirements funded did not vary significantly over the period until FY 2002 and that the percentage of authorized positions filled since FY 1996 has varied between 90 and 100.

**Figure A.7**
**Manpower and Personnel Ratios for Security Forces**

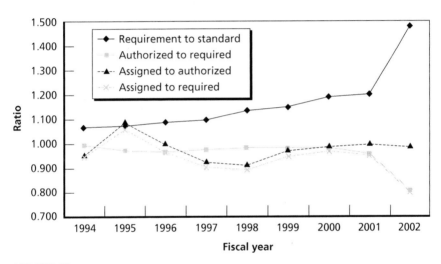

# References

AETC—*See* Air Education and Training Command.

Air Education and Training Command, *AETC Strategic Plan: FY2003–2004*, December 2002a.

———, *Air Education and Training Command 2002 Stakeholders Report: A Snapshot of AETC: The First Command*, 2002b.

Armstrong, Bruce, and S. Craig Moore, *Air Force Manpower, Personnel, and Training: Roles and Interactions*, Santa Monica, Calif.: RAND Corporation, R-2429-AF, 1980.

Ausink, John, Jonathan K. Cave, and Manuel J. Carrillo, *Background and Theory Behind the Compensations, Accessions, and Personnel (CAPM) Model*, Santa Monica, Calif.: RAND Corporation, MR-1667-AF/OSD, 2003.

Becker, Brian E., David Ulrich, and Mark A. Huselid, *The HR Scorecard: Linking People, Strategy, and Performance,* Cambridge, Mass.: Harvard Business School Press, 2001.

DAF—*See* Department of the Air Force.

Dahlman, Carl J., Robert Kerchner, and David E. Thaler, *Setting Requirements for Maintenance Manpower in the U.S. Air Force*, Santa Monica, Calif.: RAND Corporation, MR-1436-AF, 2002.

Davis, Paul, *Analytic Architecture for Capabilities-Based Planning, Mission-System Analysis, and Transformation*, Santa Monica, Calif.: RAND Corporation, MR-1513-OSD, 2002.

Department of the Air Force, *Military Promotion and Demotion*, Air Force Policy Directive 36-25, June 21, 1993a.

———, *Trained Personnel Requirements*, Air Force Instruction 36-2616, December 10, 1993b.

———, *Security Police Squadrons*, Air Force Manpower Standard 43XX, December 12, 1994.

———, *Fuels Management*, Air Force Manpower Standard 41D1, May 3, 1996.

———, *Readiness*, Air Force Policy Directive 10-2, March 1, 1997a.

———, *Explosive Ordnance Disposal (EOD) Flight*, Air Force Manpower Standard 44ED, March 7, 1997b.

———, *Readiness Flight*, Air Force Manpower Standard 44EB, March 9, 2000.

———, *USAF Almanac*, May 2002a.

———, *Aerospace Expeditionary Force Planning*, Air Force Instruction 10-400, October 16, 2002b.

———, *Personnel Strategic Plan, Fiscal Year 2004–2009*, 2003a.

———, *Assignments*, Air Force Instruction 36-2110, June 9, 2003b.

———, *Battle Staff Operation*, Air Force Instruction 10-201, December 12, 2003c.

———, *Determining Manpower Requirements*, Air Force Instruction 38-201, December 30, 2003d.

———, *Total Force Development*, Air Force Policy Directive 36-26, January 1, 2004a.

———, *Air Force Training Program*, Vol. 2: *Training Management*, Air Force Instruction 36-2201, January 13, 2004b.

Doyle, John C., Bruce A. Francis, and Allen R. Tannenbaum, *Feedback Control Theory*, New York: MacMillan Publishing Company, 1990.

GAO—*See* Government Accountability Office.

Galway, Lionel A., Richard J. Buddin, Michael Thirtle, Peter Ellis, and Judith D. Mele, *Understrength Air Force Career Fields: A Force Management Approach*, Santa Monica, Calif.: RAND Corporation, MG-131-AF, 2005.

Government Accountability Office, *DoD Competitive Sourcing*, Washington, D.C., GAO-01-907T, June 28, 2001.

———, *A Model of Strategic Human Capital Management*, Washington, D.C., GAO-02-373SP, March 2002.

Hosek, James, R., Michael G. Mattock, Carol Fair, Jennifer Kavanagh, Jennifer Sharp, and Mark Totten, *Attracting the Best: How the Military Competes for Information Personnel*, Santa Monica, Calif.: RAND Corporation, MG-108-OSD, 2004.

Jumper, John, *Chief's Sight Picture: Officer Force Development—Spreading the Word*, October 7, 2003. Online at http://www.af.mil/media/viewpoints/force_development.html (as of May 2005).

Lengnick-Hall, Cynthia A., and Mark L. Lengnick-Hall, *Human Resource Management in the Knowledge Economy*, San Francisco: Berrett-Koehler Publishers, Inc., 2002.

Office of Personnel Management, *Human Capital Assessment and Accountability Framework*, last updated 2006. Online at http://apps.opm.gov/HumanCapital/tool/index.cfm (as of May 26, 2005).

OPM—*See* Office of Personnel Management.

Robbert, Albert A., Brent R. Keltner, Kenneth Reynolds, Mark Spranca, Beth A. Benjamin, and Elizabeth Benjamin, *Differentiation in Military Human Resource Management*, Santa Monica, Calif.: RAND Corporation, MR-838-OSD, 1997.

Senge, Peter M., et al., *The Fifth Discipline Fieldbook*, New York: Doubleday/Currency, 1994.

Simon, Herbert A., *Models of Man: Social and Rational*, New York: John Wiley and Sons, Inc., 1957.

Ulrich, Dave, "Intellectual Capital = Competence x Commitment," in James W. Cortada and John A. Woods, eds., *The Knowledge Management Yearbook 1999–2000*, Boston: Butterworth Heinemann, 1999, pp. 126–138.

U.S. Code, Title 10, Section 115, Personnel Strengths: Requirement for Annual Authorization, March 18, 2004.

U.S. Code, Title 10, Section 691, Permanent End Strength Levels to Support Two Major Regional Contingencies, March 18, 2004.